ROBIN

MW00488079

SECOND EDITION

MOVING TO CHARLESTON

THE UN-TOURIST GUIDE®

CONTENTS

Chapter 9
From Pre-K to Post Grad

Chapter 10
Making Friends and Getting Involved

Chapter 11
Practical Notebook on Moving

INTRODUCTION

WHY EVERYONE LOVES CHARLESTON

Charleston, South Carolina regularly commands the top spot on travel "favorite" lists. So far, *Condé Nast Traveler* voted her "America's Favorite City" five years in a row and "America's Friendliest City" for the last two years. *Travel + Leisure* voted her #1 City in the United States. She's also landed a *T+L* Reader's Choice designation of #1 Destination in the World.

A visitor enjoys a carriage ride down Church Street

I'd argue Charleston isn't just the best city in the world—it's the most irresistible city in the world. Like so many others, I moved here because I simply couldn't stop myself. As a free-floating writer and artist, I can work from anywhere in the world. Naturally I considered Paris, Chicago, London, Rome, San Francisco, Sonoma, and many cities famous for their quality of life. It was over a to-die-for crab cake in the courtyard of Magnolia's on East Bay that I realized no place on Earth felt like home to me as much as Charleston.

I meet people all the time who have similar stories. British designer Steven Shell drove 6,000 miles up and down the East Coast looking for the perfect American town in which to anchor his family and his business. He simply got out of the car here and didn't get back in it. The same thing happened to Donatella and Giulio Della Porta, owners of The Hidden Countship, who decided to move to Charleston from Tuscany within a half an hour of a walk through the city. Stories like these prove that a visit to Charleston is both divine and dangerous. Come for just the weekend if you dare, but keep your realtor's phone number handy.

Though I moved here from "off" as Charlestonians call it, I discovered that my 10th great grandfather, John Ashby, Esq., was one of the first cassiques sent by King Charles II to settle the new "Charles Towne". This strange twist means I am at once a "come yah," the local Gullah word for those who move here, and a "bin yah," the word for those who have been here all along.

Does moving here live up to the dream? Yes, it does. It's likely all that you're dreaming of—and more. Is it like being on vacation all the time? Yes, it is. Even a dreaded Monday morning commute involves at least a few dolphins, the wide silver ocean, spritely blue shrimp boats, moss-draped oaks and all the funny seabirds you can handle. Even if it is a Monday, we don't suffer.

Breakfast means biscuits; lunch is a salad of local John's Island vegetables, and dinner means fresh fish (and more often than not) cocktails with friends on someone's dock, patio, rooftop, or boat. Weekends are devoted to days at the beach, kayaking, paddle boarding, surfing, fishing and boating capped off by long southern-style dinners. You'll find few here devoted to Saturday chores and home improvement projects. There are too many irresistible distractions.

If the weather is good, chores can wait

Here's a secret: It's a local custom to drive straight to the beach when we've had to leave Charleston for business or family matters. The smell of the pines followed by the distinctive smell of pluff mud, that oozy brown bouillabaisse of the tidal flats, means we're home. If all that isn't enough to convince you to trade your boots for flip flops, here are a few more good reasons to move to Charleston:

Top 10 Reasons to Move to Charleston

#1 Natural Beauty – The Lowcountry has some of the most unspoiled stunning natural beauty in the United States. You'll enjoy the ocean, beach, and marshes every season of the year. Birders can choose from dozens of hot spots; water lovers have endless year-round options and hikers will enjoy miles and miles of trails through unspoiled nature reserves.

Sandy boardwalks give way to wide, uncrowded beaches

#2 Food – Charleston has some of the best restaurants in the world, and it's not all seafood either. Whether you're in shorts at a creek-side dive or in a seersucker suit at an award-winning eatery downtown, you'll find chefs who are passionate about fresh, local ingredients and real southern hospitality. If you like to cook, come to the farmer's market in Marion Square and spend your Saturday morning shopping, people watching and eating with the locals.

#3 Community – Charlestonians have a long history of hospitality and philanthropy. We are proudly the home of the largest no-kill animal shelter in the South (nearly half of Charleston households have at least one fur kid), our historic Preservation Society is the oldest in the United States, and every spring volunteers diligently walk the entire lengths of our beaches collecting trash, marking the nests of endangered loggerhead turtles and filling in sandcastle holes that could trap hatchlings. Locals are also fervently dedicated to the Buy Local movement.

FIG is one of Charleston's many farm-to-table restaurants.

#4 People – People in Charleston are happy. Forget what you've heard about Charleston high society; most Lowcountry dwellers are too busy having fun to be concerned about keeping up with the Joneses. It's implied that everyone, including houseguests, are welcome at parties. And, once you merely declare that you're moving here, don't be surprised that when your social calendar fills up so quickly that you don't have time to worry if you'll be able to make friends.

#5 Weather – If you're moving from up north, you can donate your winter gear. You'll never shovel snow again. Here you'll play on the beach, garden and enjoy life outdoors virtually year round. Summer comes early and stays late into September. Locals will show you how to adapt your wardrobe and daily rhythms to make the most of the hot months. September through December is magical as summer's heat and tourist traffic give way to cooler days, walk-in seating at world-famous restaurants, and plenty of parking at the beach.

**A rescue dog and her mom check out the art
at the Piccolo Spoleto festival**

Kayakers enjoy a paddle to Magnolia Plantation

#6 Economy – Our economy is on fire. And, Charleston's leaders are working hard to diversify it even more. The Digital Corridor initiative is responsible for Charleston's growing identity as the "Silicon Harbor", so if you're in the tech field, get here—we need you!

#7 History – As one of America's first colonies and the place where the Civil War began, Charleston has no shortage of carefully preserved historical sites. You can spend an entire lifetime wandering through buildings, museums, cemeteries, churches and military forts—and you'll still never cover everything. Charleston is unique because everywhere you look her history is as obvious and apparent as the lines of rock in geological stratum. Take a short walk downtown and you'll find streets named after indigenous Indian tribes. Turn down one of the many cobbled streets and you'll be walking over ballast stones from merchant ships. Look up and you'll spot the sharp Chevaux-de-Frise iron spikes over garden gates—remnants of the slave revolt. You'll see decorative earthquake rods inserted in historic houses and commerce still taking place at the outdoor City Market. Fragments of the old walls of the city still stand, as does the Powder Magazine, the forts where wars were started and fought, and many of the original taverns, hotels, and stables. Though Charleston has long progressed from banning atheists, the diverse and numerous houses of worship abide, giving the Charleston it's nickname—the Holy City.

#8 Manners – "Ma'am" and "Sir" are still the preferred addresses between people of all ages, races and backgrounds. For example, if you're in New York City you might get away with asking "Hey, where's the closest ATM?" but in Charleston, you'll need to begin your exchanges with "Excuse me (Ma'am or Sir)", no matter the age, race or occupation of the person to whom you're speaking. If you don't, you'll still get a friendly answer, but you won't blend in or enjoy the perks of interactions that begin with respect.

#9 Style – A constant parade of straw hats, bow ties, seersucker suits and floor-grazing sundresses means style is alive and well in Charleston. Obvious designer labels are a faux pas, as is any overt show of wealth. Ladies wear skirts or dresses and men wear shirts with collars. Wearing black is verboten unless attending a funeral. Far from being an oppressive social obligation, Charleston's smart sense of colorful, functional and polite style is one of the things to love most about living here.

**Local Jasper Brown shows Charleston how to dress
Courtesy L.E. Sykes Photography, Jasper Brown
and Charleston Shop Curator**

Surf's up on Isle of Palms

#10 Active Lifestyle – If you've been grinding away in a dark northern gym, you're going to love living here. Most people begin the day with a long walk on the beach or in the neighborhood (dog leading the way) and bike wherever they don't have to drive. Weekends find fitness devotees on long walks in beautiful historic neighborhoods, running or walking over the formidable Ravenel Bridge, or engaging in some kind of water sport that burns off our substantial brunches.

CHAPTER 1

A BRIEF HISTORY OF CHARLESTON

Four thousand years before our story starts, the Kiawah, Etiwan, Edisto, Stono and other tribes thrived along the shores of the Lowcountry. The indigenous people who called this land home played a big role in Charleston's birth and growth, but our story really gets started in 1521 when the Spanish landed on the banks of the Ashley River. They were the first outsiders who attempted to settle the land—but weren't the last to limp home with only a handful left alive. Of the first 500 Spanish settlers, only 150 returned home. In 1563 the French Huguenots fared about the same in their settlement attempt.

In 1629 King Charles I of England gave Sir Robert Heath the entire "Province of Carolina," or what we know as North and South Carolina. Sir Robert had about as much luck as the Spanish and French, so the king unfriended him and stripped him of his responsibilities. Decades later King Charles II made one more run at the New World. He gave the land to eight of his loyal friends, whom he called the Lords Proprietors. These English settlers created a functional settlement on Albemarle Point on the Ashley River, then eventually move across the river and create our beloved "Charles Town".

In 1670 English settlers from Bermuda, Barbados and Virginia joined the British pioneers—but soon discovered their new town was vulnerable to Spanish, Indian, French and pirate attacks. (Even then, everyone loved Charleston!) In order to bump up the population and better defend the city, the governor declared everyone was welcome in his new town…except atheists. As a result, Charles Town became a delightful amalgamation of ethnicities and a safe haven for French

Huguenots and Sephardic Jews. By 1770, the town had grown to the fourth largest port in the colonies and was second in wealth only to Philadelphia.

By 1770, more than half of the 11,000 people in the city were imported African, Indian and Caribbean slaves, and Charles Town was one of the largest slave trading ports in the colonies. Slaves were unloaded in a quarantine area and kept in "pest houses" on Sullivan's Island before being sold at public markets. This massive slave labor population was the driving force behind the enormous inland and riverside plantations that grew rice and indigo. In town, as a result of the governor's open-door policy, nearly every religious denomination was well represented by an impressive house of worship—and Charles Town began to take shape as the Holy City.

Things took a fateful turn in 1774 when South Carolina declared its independence from England on the steps of the Exchange. The American Revolution soon followed and bloody battles were fought in and around the Lowcountry. The British managed to occupy the city between 1780 and 1782, but finally, thanks to the efforts of fierce militiamen like Francis "Swamp Fox" Marion, they gave up. Residents quickly rechristened their city "Charleston."

In 1793 the invention of the cotton gin made wealthy Charleston plantation owners even wealthier. (How wealthy? Spend a night at opulent Wentworth Mansion and see for yourself!) South Carolina quickly became the largest exporter of cotton. The influx of money allowed the rich to spend summers away from the malarial rivers and marshes on hot plantations and take up residence in luxurious mansions and townhouses on the tip of the peninsula. Here sea breezes cooled the grand two-story piazzas where high society members were strategically staged for an endless procession of parties and soirees. In the kitchens and fields, black Charlestonians spoke Gullah, a linguistic gumbo of African, French, German, Jamaican, English, Bahamian and Dutch. Because the law allowed slaves to buy their freedom, there were a few free blacks running successful enterprises. Free African American Jehu Jones ran a successful retreat on Sullivan's Island, a tailoring business on Broad Street and another hotel in Charleston. For slaves, things went from horrible to really horrible one night in 1822 when plans for a massive slave revolt werediscovered. Fear of an uprising led to pandemonium and hysteria in white society, and free and enslaved blacks suffered tighter restrictions than ever before.

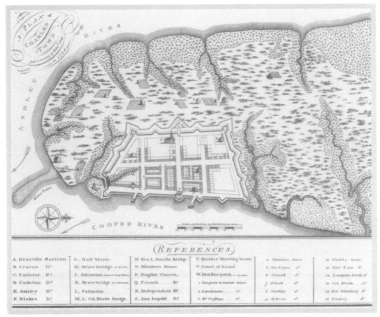

A Plan of Charles Town from a survey of Edwd. Crisp in 1704
Courtesy U.S. Library of Congress

The hysteria never quite died down, but the planter class still reigned until the 1860s when the ever-widening gap between the North and South finally became a violent chasm. Though President Lincoln wouldn't admit it until much later, the rift was all about slavery. In 1860 South Carolina was the first state to secede from the Union, and in 1861 Captain George James fired the first shot of the Civil War at Fort Sumter from a boat in the harbor. On January 1, 1863 President Lincoln issued his final Emancipation Proclamation, freeing all slaves that were not in states under Union control. Because slavery was such an important part of Southern commerce, Confederate soldiers dug in until President Andrew Johnson declared the war over on August 20th, 1866 and they were forced to concede. For Charleston, it wasn't just the end of a war; it was the end of an era. For newly free blacks, the struggle for equality had just begun.

Without slave labor, Charleston's enormous plantations couldn't operate at a profit. For the planter class, the days of ease and wealth were over. The city endured a mass exodus and nearly 20 years of reconstruction. Just as the last bit of plaster and paint dried, the city was nearly wiped off the map by an earthquake. On August 31, 1886, a quake measuring 7.6 on the Richter scale nearly leveled Charleston and was felt as far away as Cuba and Bermuda. The Holy City was slowly rebuilt, but not for the last time.

Hibernian Hall after the 1886 earthquake
Courtesy University of Saint Louis archives

At the turn of the century, abandoned rice irrigation infrastructure was already rotting on now-quiet plantations. Sharecroppers and landowners had turned from rice and indigo to cotton, but by 1920 the boll weevil had destroyed what was left of the cotton industry. Many workers simply packed up and headed north to find work in industry.

Despite the economic struggles that took place between the Roaring 20s and the end of World War II, Charleston's artistic community thrived and contributed to the 'Southern Renaissance'. There was tension between New South and Old South ideals, and some of that tension remains today. In the throes of this low-grade social tension,

Charleston struggled through the Great Depression, a slow but surprisingly peaceful desegregation, and the economic dead zones of the 1970s and early 80s. By the late 80s, the city was once again ready for a renaissance. However, Mother Nature had other ideas and turned her sites on the Holy City. On September 21st, 1989 Hurricane Hugo made landfall in Charleston Harbor causing $10 billion worth of destruction, damaging over 75% of Charleston's historic district, ripping apart neighboring towns and leveling islands. At the time, it was the most expensive storm ever recorded in the United States.

King Street, looking north, Charleston, S.C., between 1910 and 1920
Courtesy U.S. Library of Congress

After Hugo, Charleston rebuilt once again. Tourism and new industry infused the economy; with great effort the city's magnificent architecture was saved and her islands and neighborhoods restored. The economic downturn of the early 2000's took a toll on real estate sales, but Charleston has clearly rebounded. For Charlestonians and all who endeavor to call her home, the future looks bright.

Still, history lives in the hearts of her people. Though it rarely comes up in polite company, "come yahs" from the north refer to the War Between the States as the "Civil War", but don't be surprised if "been yah" Charlestonians refer to it as "the War of Northern Aggression", or even "The Recent Unpleasantness", as if Charleston's vast plantation wealth was lost only yesterday. Gullah is still spoken, sea grass baskets still woven, collected, and proudly displayed, and Gullah cuisine abounds.

Though Charleston's history was often chaotic and checkered, through devastation and adversity she's evolved and grown into a peaceful, gracious city with a small-town feel. Everyone is still welcome in this glorious place. And, there's no better time than the present to enjoy her new Belle Époque.

Window boxes with "thrillers, fillers, and spillers" adorn Church Street

CHAPTER 2

QUICK GEOGRAPHIC GUIDE

For all the publicity it gets, the city of Charleston is a relatively small place. With roughly 128,000 residents, it's ranked as the 199th largest city in North America. However, Charleston is one of the fastest growing cities in the nation. The Charleston region includes the peninsula, an area of only 97 square miles, and the 27 cities and towns that makeup Charleston, Dorchester and Berkeley counties. This book covers the most popular places to live, including Charleston, Mount Pleasant, West Ashley, Sullivan's Island, Isle of Palms, Daniel Island, James Island, Johns Island, Kiawah Island, Seabrook Island, Dewees Island, Summerville, and Folly Beach.

Roughly 750,000 residents live in three counties that make up an area of just over 3,000 square miles. Getting around the Charleston area is very easy most days. But, in bad weather or periods of high tourist traffic it can be a bit confounding. Locals are good-natured about tourist traffic in high season, and you will be too. After all, visitors must return home, but you get to stay in paradise.

Getting Around by Car

Interstate 26 is the main thoroughfare leading into the area. It runs southeast from Landrum, South Carolina right into the heart of Charleston. Interstate 526, or the Mark Clark Expressway, forms a half circle around the region and spans Mount Pleasant to West Ashley. Highway 17, or the Coastal Highway, runs north from Virginia along the coast and through Charleston, ending in Punta Gorda, Florida.

Courtesy Charleston Regional Development Alliance

Getting to Know Charleston Communities

Charleston Peninsula

Living on the Charleston peninsula means living in one of the most beautiful historical settings in the U.S. The peninsula is a finger of land pointing south into the Charleston Harbor. The Ashley River runs along the eastern bank and the Cooper River runs along the western bank. Both rivers and the Wando River empty into Charleston Harbor, a busy but picturesque commercial port that gives way to the Atlantic Ocean.

One of the many historic homes south of Broad Street
Photo courtesy of Jason Crichton Photography

The Charleston peninsula is home to 130,113 residents and its biggest draw is the chance to spend each day immersed in the city's incredible history. Every street is beautiful, filled with charm and full of stories. Residents are within walking distance to nearby restaurants, shops, two large grocery stores, and several small corner stores. Real estate choices range from lavish mansions and homes in the famous South of Broad historic district to narrow Charleston Single Houses, small cottages, carriage houses, and character-filled apartments above stores. There are several condominium complexes on the peninsula, most with fantastic water views.

Fewer addresses in the country are more prestigious than those South of Broad Street. Real estate on the tip of the peninsula is not for the faint of heart, but well worth shelling out if you can manage it. An 800-square-foot, one bed, one bath slice of a historic building will set you back about $500,000—and that's about as cheap as it gets. If you want a single-family home or a historic mansion, be prepared to part with millions. Be warned, there are strict policies about what you can and cannot change about these historic homes. It's best to go into South-of-Broad real estate thinking of yourself more as a caretaker than an owner.

North of Broad, restored historic houses will still set you back a million or more, but there are plenty of affordable, neglected properties just waiting for someone to love them back to their glory. Many Charleston single houses have either been handed down from generation to generation or been converted to housing for College of Charleston students or apartments. As a result, North of Broad housing can have a grittier feel. North of Broad is still safe, convenient, and quaint, and residents have a fierce, proud love for their neighborhoods.

Mount Pleasant

Friendly Mount Pleasant is Charleston's more affordable, eclectic neighbor. From the peninsula, cross the mighty Ravenel Bridge headed east and you'll enter one of America's best seaside towns. This is a safe, laid-back, affordable place that has plenty of shopping, restaurants, and activities within walking and biking distance and fast access to beaches. With a 2016 population of 78,944 residents in 41 square miles, Mount Pleasant has a little bit of everything for homebuyers. Home prices depend on the quality of the house, the neighborhood, and proximity to the water.

Locals buy fish right off the boat at Mount Pleasant Seafood

Mount Pleasant is a grab bag of historic homes, 1950s bungalows, new-since Hurricane-Hugo subdivisions and brand new condos and townhouses. You can buy a basic two bedroom, one bath condo for around $120,000—and many "rice birds" do just that and call Mount P. home for the winter. Custom homes, homes with significant square footage, historic homes in Old Village, and water views can take you into the millions.

Isle of Palms and Wild Dunes

In summer, vacationers flock to the many beach house rentals on this fun-loving barrier island. Head across the connector bridge from Mount Pleasant onto Isle of Palms and you'll notice this island looks a bit different than the others. Hugo leveled it in 1989, and, as a result, you won't find many historic homes or tall trees here. What you will find are plenty of five to eight bedroom houses, mostly summer rentals, which are either directly on the beach or just steps away. The "IOP" has a population of roughly 4,000 people on 5.6 square miles of low-lying sandy soil. There is one grocery store on the island and a few restaurants on Ocean Boulevard and in the Wild Dunes complex.

Isle of Palms new beachfront homes stay busy through the summer
Photo courtesy Jason Crichton Photography

The Wild Dunes resort at the northern tip of the island is 1,600 acres of hotel, condo, and timeshare properties. IOP and Wild Dunes properties range from $500,000 to $5 million, but you can get a six-week share of a three bedroom, three bath ocean-view condo for $100,000.

Summer on the IOP feels like one long beach party with an ever-changing guest list. Living here means you won't have to fight for beach parking, but you will have to endure slow traffic crossing the two-lane Isle of Palms Connector Bridge during peak times. You may also have to share your front or back yard easement with beach goers who are allowed to park along one side of any street as long as they don't block gates or driveways.

Sullivan's Island

Quiet, historic, and slightly overgrown, Sullivan's Island is home to many contiguous generations of locals. While Isle of Palms attracts vacationers with its plentiful beach rentals, there are very few rentals and no hotels or B&Bs on Sullivan's Island. To get here, cross the swing bridge from Mount Pleasant or the span bridge that connects it to the IOP.

Sullivan's Island is the local's island
Photo courtesy Jason Crichton Photography

This tiny barrier island is just 3.3 square miles and is home to just 1,875 residents. Hugo mostly spared the island so you'll find older homes here, especially on the southern tip of the island by Fort Moultrie. Sometimes lucky house hunters can find a fixer or one bedroom, one bath apartment in a larger house for around $600,000—but a four bedroom, three bath house will set you back around $3 million. Sullivan's Island beaches have no public amenities and the wind and waves tend to be a bit stronger here—so tourist traffic is lighter in the summer and virtually non-existent off-season.

Daniel Island

Sparkly-new, pastel-painted Daniel Island is the very picture of modern island life. Across the Cooper River to the east of the peninsula is a 4,000-acre island, once privately owned by the Guggenheim Foundation. Daniel Island is a master-planned community of neighborhoods, parks, schools, lakes, trails, shops, and restaurants. There is a private country club and golf course as well as the Family Circle Tennis Center and Blackbaud Stadium. House hunters who prefer new construction to historic preservation fall hard for Daniel Island. The island is astonishingly beautiful and manages to retain some of the deliciously mysterious vistas traditional to the Deep South. Whether you buy a three-bedroom home for $300,000 or 5,000 square foot mini-mansion for $3 million (there are options in between), you'll be 15 minutes from the beach and downtown Charleston and within walking or biking distance to shopping and restaurants.

The island is home to herds of deer and is an important breeding and migration site for birds. Dolphins play in the river and are easily spotted from land. You may actually start looking forward to your daily jog. Note that there is also a healthy population of bats, alligators, and snakes on the island—and they are all an important part of the Lowcountry ecosystem, so you'll have to learn to co-exist.

Daniel Island has plenty of quaint eateries

Though some purists dislike Daniel Island because it lacks the authentic wear and tear of historic houses downtown, those who appreciate modern conveniences love having a beautiful Southern- style home and walk-in closets. For this reason, Daniel Island continues to be a good choice and a good investment.

Folly Beach

Just south of the peninsula, Charleston's most whimsical beach town is actually a barrier island that is home to 2,000 permanent residents in just 18 square miles. Known for its nightlife and surfable waves, Folly Beach is where visitors and locals alike go to relax. Compared to the other islands, real estate here is less expensive but more bohemian. You can spend $2 million on a beach house here, but if you don't mind living small and simply, you can land a 600-square foot beach cottage for under $350,000.

**Folly Beach is popular late-night fun spot for locals and vacationers
Photo by Brian Stansberry**

West Ashley

No matter where you choose to live, you'll find yourself running errands in über-convenient West Ashley at some point. Just across the river to the south from the peninsula, this little offshoot of Charleston grew up in the 1950s and is now enjoying a modern renaissance. What it lacks in visual appeal (compared to its Cinderella sister, Charleston) it makes up for in retail indulgences and affordability. With a proper mall, a mega cinema and all the big-box stores you could want, the town's 60,000 residents enjoy a booming business scene along with close proximity to beaches and downtown Charleston. Enormous houses on generous tracts of land can be had for $1 to $2 million and small 1950s bungalows can be yours for under $200,000. All in all, West Ashley is a great value. If you can sacrifice a little historic curb appeal, you can have a Charleston address without the Charleston price.

James Island

South of the peninsula and inshore from Folly Beach, James Island is home to 11,500 residents. It's hard to say how big the official town is because long-running incorporation battles produced an incomprehensible zoning map. Regardless of your official address, living here will put you within 15 minutes of Folly Beach and downtown Charleston. You'll likely have to drive to do business with restaurants and grocery stores; however, James Island real estate is a great buy and a good location. Despite its proximity to one of the most popular beaches on the coasts, you can still find a three bedroom, three-bath ocean front condo for under $500,000—and you can spend less for a house of the same size without the water view.

John's Island

Semi-rural John's Island is Charleston's own farm town. This 84-square mile barrier island lies south of James Island and inland of Seabrook and Kiawah Islands and is a sanctuary for nearly 14,000 residents. The island is known for its small farms that produce much of the produce found at regional farmer's markets and local restaurants. Wildlife on John's Island is wonderfully diverse. If you'd like to start your own micro-farm, there is still plenty of undeveloped land. You can buy a four-bedroom, three-bath house for under $300,000. But, if want water views, you can spend up to $3,000,000 on a similar house.

Kiawah Island

Lush Kiawah Island is located 15 miles south of the peninsula. Most of this small island is a gated resort with just 475 families living in 11 square miles. Hugo ignored Kiawah so the island still features majestic live oaks and miles of undisturbed natural beauty. Though just 15 miles from downtown Charleston, the winding drive takes about 45 minutes. Like Sullivan's Island, you can find some older homes in the $600,000 range but most houses here are large, luxurious, and occupied by celebrities and high-earners who exchange big bucks for lots of privacy.

Seabrook Island

Small but mighty Seabrook Island is a seven-square mile stretch of natural beauty. There are no hotels and the island's 1200 residents live quietly. Ambitious house hunters who don't mind fixers can find a three bedroom, two bath condo under 1000 square feet for under $250,000. You may not get a lot of living space for the money on Seabrook, but you will get gorgeous water views and a peaceful house just steps from the beach.

Dewees Island

Private, eco-friendly Dewees Island is a red herring on the real estate scene. It's only accessible by ferry (your name has to be on the guest list) and there are no cars permitted. Dewees sports just 63 houses on 1,200 acres. Residents who live here commit to strict earth-saving bylaws, shuttle kids to school via ferry and live close to the water and the land. Home prices range from $35,000 for a partial year share to $2 million for a single-family home. If you've dreamed of running away and living a far simpler life, Dewees might just be what you're looking for.

Awendaw

About 1,200 people live in this small eight square mile fishing community. Awendaw is often overlooked because it doesn't seem as convenient to Charleston as other neighborhoods. But, smart house hunters realize it's close enough. You can buy a four bedroom, four-bath house on a generous parcel of land for just over $300,000. Here you'll have fast access to the Bull Island Ferry, a great public marina and lots of secret fishing holes.

Summerville

Forty-five thousand people call bustling Summerville home. Situated on 18 square miles of land, this small town works hard to retain its southern charm while going gangbusters with economic development. Summerville is a 30-minute drive from Charleston and her beaches, but the $250,000 average price tag for a very decent three bedroom, three bath home might be enough to lure you west.

North Charleston, Park Circle, and Mixson

As Charleston's grittier, more industrialized sister, North Charleston is home to 108,000 people in 76 square miles—and the massive Boeing assembly plant. This city is trying to improve, but still has some work to do. While it's home to four-star hotels, a major music venue and plenty of commerce, North Charleston has the unfortunate designation of having a crime index of just "4"—meaning that it's safer than only 3% of the other cities in the United States. Despite the sketchy rep, family homes of 1,800 square feet or more range from $250,000 to $500,000.

Worth mentioning—and investigating—are the neighborhoods of Mixson and Park Circle. Park Circle is the heart of revitalization efforts in North Charleston, and it also has the most affordable housing closest to downtown. While some areas seem semi-dodgy, North Charleston still has a lower crime rate than standard cities like Indianapolis and Santa Fe. Park Circle has a fierce little community that is passionately working to make positive changes, and is home to some of the most respected and popular restaurants in Charleston. While you're in Park Circle, be sure to check out the funky Mixson neighborhood. Mixson homes are green (environmentally friendly) and thoughtfully designed. There are shops and restaurants within walking and biking distance. Plus, there always seems to be something fun happening. Whatever is going on in Mixson, it's good for North Charleston and you may want to investigate joining in.

Getting Around Town

For the most part, two-lane bridges and roads network the Charleston area. Historic streets can be narrow and parking can be scarce outside of a parking garage (there are plenty). For these reasons, locals tend to bike or walk wherever they can. Golf carts are a popular option as they are legal on secondary roads as long as you're no more than two miles from home.

The Charleston Area Regional Transportation Authority (CARTA) bus system runs throughout downtown, Mount Pleasant, James Island, West Ashley and North Charleston. Buses are bike-friendly and loading up just takes seconds. Transit is accessible with lifts for wheelchairs and buses that "kneel" or lower at the curb. Service animals are welcomed and there are special low fares for riders with disabilities.

Charleston also has a handy hop-on-hop-off DASH trolley system that is free and stops at all the major sites downtown. Locals love the trolley system for house guest YOYO (You're On Your Own) days: You can drop your guests at a stop in the morning, let them run around town all day on the trolley, then pick them up in the afternoon when they're tuckered out.

Bicycle taxis are a fun way to get around Charleston
Courtesy Nickie Cutrona Photography

For a city of its size, Charleston has a decent number of taxis. However, your best bet is to call one directly rather than hail on the street. Charleston Green Taxi and their eco-friendly fleet of Prius cars provide reliable service to and from wherever you want to go. Charleston recently joined the Uber network and you can now find a private driver via the popular Uber app.

In town, there are plenty of bicycle taxis (called pedicabs or rickshaws) that can take two people around the peninsula. Bicycle taxi drivers from Charleston Rickshaw and Charleston Pedicab are friendly and happy to make recommendations or give commentary.

DASH trollies are free and stop at all the major sites

Getting Out of Town

Charleston International Airport (CHS) is small, efficient, and easily navigable. If you're used to an enormous international airport, CHS will be a bit of a change, though the recent $189 million renovation resulted in the modern aesthetic and convinces of bigger larger international airports. There are direct flights to and from 21 airports and 16 cities, but you'll likely go through Charlotte or Atlanta en route to everywhere else. In true Charleston style, Ambassadors in blue vests will help you with anything you need. It's safe to say that each of the 2.6 million passengers that pass through CHS each year always get a warm farewell and a warmer welcome home.

Nonstop flights available to and from CHS:

- Atlanta
- Baltimore
- Boston
- Chicago
- Charlotte
- Cincinnati
- Dallas /Ft. Worth

- Detroit
- Ft. Lauderdale
- Houston
- Memphis
- Miami
- Minneapolis
- Nashville
- New York City (JFK / LGA)
- Newark
- Philadelphia
- Seattle
- Washington DC (DCA / IAD)

CHAPTER 3

THE CLIMATE AND THE ENVIRONMENT

Charleston has a humid subtropical climate that is characterized by mild winters, hot, humid summers, and regular rainfall. From June through September thunderstorms are frequent (and welcome), with occasional rain the rest of the year. We enjoy an average of 230 days of sunshine a year, and the region stays warm through November. Charleston winters are short and easy with an average low of 50 F in December, January, and February. Highs peak in July at 88 F (annual average) and lows bottom out in January at 43 F (annual average).

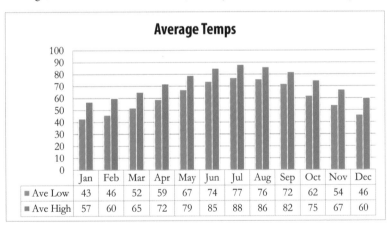

Average Temps

	Jan	Feb	Mar	Apr	May	Jun	Jul	Aug	Sep	Oct	Nov	Dec
■ Ave Low	43	46	52	59	67	74	77	76	72	62	54	46
■ Ave High	57	60	65	72	79	85	88	86	82	75	67	60

One of the most frequently asked questions about moving to Charleston is: "Is it really that hot?" Charleston really isn't that hot. It's just more humid than what most people are used to. Locals combat steamy days with loose clothing, frequent trips to the beach and liberal use of air conditioning.

We don't change our wardrobe very much with the seasons. Sweaters and sweatshirts are the perfect match for shorts or cotton pants, and boots and tights warm up ladies' short summer dresses. If you wear the right clothes, Charleston has a very agreeable climate.

Charleston Seasons and Weather

If you're moving to Charleston from up north, you can leave your wool sweaters, gloves, and ski jackets behind. (If you want a laugh, or a good deal on skis and jackets, stop by a local Goodwill store!)

Spring

Spring signals the return of the beloved Farmer's Market. From March until June we open the windows and enjoy the sea breeze and the cacophony of migrating birds. Though we have plenty of evergreens all year, spring comes early and brings plenty of flowers, warblers, and warm breezes.

Spring signals the return of the Farmer's Market

Summer

In June, we head to the beach to cool off after work and on weekends. Tourists and houseguests arrive en mass. Locals take to secret beaches and watering holes or just join the throng and enjoy the party.

Charlestonians really do welcome tourists

Fall

If summer in Charleston is a magnificent party where everyone is welcome, fall is an intimate gathering of good friends. October is the beginning of oyster roast season and locals look for any excuse to throw or attend a backyard gathering of new and old friends. Smart houseguests delay their visit until oyster season when they can tag along to one laid-back house party after another. If you love Charleston in spring and summer, you'll be hopelessly smitten in fall.

Oyster roasts are a favorite social activity in Fall
Photo courtesy Jason Crichton Photography

Winter

December is a magical time to be in Charleston and locals start celebrating the holidays on December 1st. The city is decked out with lights and there are festivities almost every night. December is usually warm, with temperatures occasionally in the mid-70s. January and February are colder and quieter and many locals choose these months to vacation out of town.

Hurricanes

Historically, hurricanes and tropical storms tend to miss Charleston. The season lasts from June 1st to November 30th every year, but in the last century only 28 tropical cyclones have made landfall here. Hurricanes Hazel (1954) and Hugo (1989) were category 4 storms and there have been three category 3 storms, including Matthew in 2016, an unnamed event in 1945, and Hurricane Gracie in 1959.

Though hurricanes and tropical storms are scarce in Charleston, you'll want to keep a hurricane kit handy and have an evacuation plan ready just in case. The Charleston County Emergency Management Department has a printable PDF that includes everything you need to know about preparing for and staying safe in a hurricane.

Even the sea turtles on Isle of Palms get into the holiday spirit

Critters

Charleston has a handful of reptiles, amphibians and insects you may not be used to. Southerners love to tell tall tales, so when it comes to whatever you've heard about alligators and Palmetto bugs, take it with a grain of salt. The fact is, our reptiles, amphibians, and insects are interesting and critical to our ecosystem and you'll rarely see anything venomous. It's easy to establish a "you-stay-over-there-and-I'll-stay-over-here" relationship with our more misunderstood residents, but it is important that you educate yourself about alligator and snake habitats and how to avoid trouble.

CHAPTER 4

LIVING WELL IN CHARLESTON

Cost of Living

The cost of living in Charleston is about 12% higher than the national average[1]. Sure, you can spend millions on a beachfront house or historic mansion, but you can also find affordable single-family homes, townhouses, and condominiums just minutes from downtown and the beach under $200,00 (and lower).

For example, in Mount Pleasant a three bedroom, three-bathroom Craftsman-style townhouse in the much-desired Marais neighborhood will cost you upwards of $500,000 with $2,400 average taxes and $390 for all utilities. Just a few hundred yards away, you can buy a basic one bedroom, one bathroom condo in Long Grove for around $150,000 with $280 for utilities. Both are three minutes from the Isle of Palms beach and both are walking distance to shops and restaurants.

In 2016, the median house sale price was $269,000 in Charleston, Mount Pleasant's median was $398,500 and the median for Sullivan's Island was $1,600,900.

---

1   www.areavibes.com/charleston-sc/cost-of-living

Mount Pleasant's Marais townhouse subdivision is one of the most sought-after addresses in Charleston

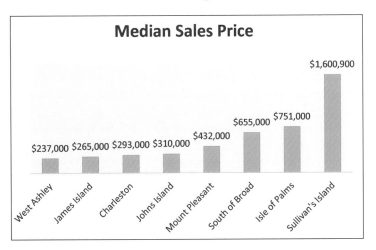

Though many transplants find that though the cost of living is higher than what they're used to, there are hundreds of ways that living in Charleston is actually cheaper than wherever you are now. For example, a day at the beach is free. You can catch your own crab, shrimp, and fish to supplement vegetables and fruit grown in your year-round garden. Our moderate climate means you can cancel your gym membership and exercise outdoors. Watching birds on the marsh, walking on the beach or wandering historic streets downtown is more fun than cable TV service. Many community activities such as Friday Night Art Walks and outdoor movies in the park are free.

And, if you don't own a boat, kayak, paddleboard or surfboard, no problem: In Charleston you're virtually guaranteed to make friends with someone who does.

Housing Choice Rule #1: Check the Flood Zone

Keep in mind that some Charleston properties are in flood zones (that's why they call it the "Lowcountry") and the extra mandatory insurance can cost up to a few hundred of dollars a month. As you're shopping, ask your agent to find out what the current zoning is for prospective properties and what the monthly cost of flood insurance would be. It's all up to FEMA's Flood Insurance Rate Map. Zones can zigzag throughout a neighborhood, so don't assume that all neighborhoods close to the water will have expensive flood insurance. It's worth checking. It's okay to fall in love with a house in a flood zone. I did and many people do, but you'll want to figure the extra expense into your budget. Note that when you visit the FEMA website you'll have to read the PDF tutorial about how to make your own map. If you're tempted to skip this tedious step, keep in mind that realtors, home sellers and insurance agents could be too, and their lack of knowledge can be very expensive for you down the road. Make yourself a big glass of sweet tea and take time to become your own flood zone expert.

What Do The Flood Zones Mean?

Charleston's local government website has a handy chart that explains all of the zones, and you'll want to become familiar with them before you start shopping. Keep in mind that high-risk (expensive insurance) areas are Zones V and VE.

If you choose a condo, townhouse, or a neighborhood with amenities, be sure to ask about regime fees. Commonly called homeowners association (HOA) or property owner's association (POA) dues, these fees can be as low as $50 a month or can skyrocket into the hundreds. Insurance and regime fees can take up a sizeable chunk of your monthly housing budget, so make sure they're part of your plan before you make an offer on a property.

Median Sales Price for Charleston homes compared to desirable areas around the country:

Source: Trulia.com

- Atlanta, Georgia – $260,000272,000
- Evanston, Illinois – $421,500340,000
- San Francisco, California – $945,0001,135,000
- Miami, Florida – $215,300269,500
- Washington, DC – $500549,000
- Boston, Massachusetts – $480,500437,500
- Cincinnati, Ohio – $131,30047,00

Utilities

Electricity

Charleston residents pay a little more for electricity than most other areas of the country—but much less than in New England and Mid-Atlantic states. The main electricity provider for the area is South Carolina Energy & Gas (SCE&G) and 70% of residents heat and cool their home with electricity[2]. The average single-family home electric bill is $155 per month, which is 35% higher than the national average. To help residents reduce their bills, SCE&G offers online tools that analyze electricity use then suggests ways to cut down energy consumption. They will also perform a free Home Energy Checkup on request. There are various rebates available for installing energy efficient infrastructure as well as assistance programs for those in need.

Natural Gas & Propane

Charlestonians use natural gas and propane, but you won't find many buried gas lines. Instead you'll see white tanks tucked under porches and behind houses. These tanks fuel water heaters, kitchen appliances, and fireplaces. Having access to natural gas or propane heat and power is a plus when storm-related power outages occur. Blue Flame is the main provider of natural gas in the Charleston area and prices have

2   www.city-data.com/city/Charleston-South-Carolina.html

been steadily dropping for a few years. As of 2014, natural gas was $2.25 per MBTU.

Water & Sewer

Charleston Water System services all three counties for water and sewer. Our drinking water comes from the Bushy Park Reservoir in Berkeley County and the Edisto River in Dorchester County. It is treated at the Hanahan Water Treatment Plant. Charleston Water System produces a water quality report every May, and the quality is high except for high lead count (likely due to the number of old homes in the area with lead pipes). Your water and sewer bill will depend on whether you live inside or outside the city, the size of your water connection, and how much you use per month.

Property Taxes

Charleston has one of the lowest per capita property tax rates in the country.

Comparing Median Property Tax Paid on Homes Across the Nation:
(Data from TaxFoundation.org)

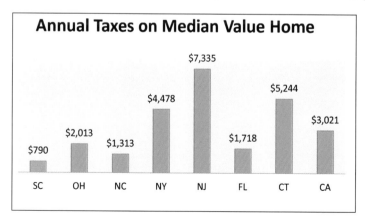

You can get answers to all your tax questions at CharlestonCounty.org.

CHAPTER 5
SERVICES

How Safe is Charleston?

Charleston has a low crime rate and falls below the national average for all types of crime. It is much safer than most cities of similar size. Even North Charleston, where crime seems high to locals, is safer than most Midwestern capital cities. In the chart below, the higher the number, the safer the neighborhood or city is.

Highest Number = Lowest Crime Rate

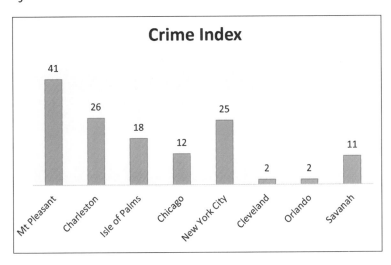

Hospitals

Healthcare costs in Charleston fall in line with the national average. The Charleston area is known for having an excellent variety of healthcare choices. Hospitals include Medical University of South Carolina (MUSC), Roper-St. Francis, East Cooper Medical Center and Trident Medical Center, among others. Rankings and patient satisfaction in descriptions below are from independent research conducted by FindTheBest.

The Medical University of South Carolina is a hub for medical academics.

MUSC is a comprehensive academic medical center ranked as the #1 hospital in South Carolina by *U.S.News & World Report,* and nationally ranked in three adult specialties and two pediatric specialties. MUSC gets the best reviews by patients in the Lowcountry and consistently has costs much lower than the national average.

Roper-St. Francis is South Carolina's only private, not-for-profit health care system. The healthcare system includes 657 beds, 90 facilities, and service in seven counties. Member hospitals include Roper Hospital, Bon Secours St. Francis Hospital, Mount Pleasant Hospital and Roper Rehabilitation Hospital. This enormous healthcare system is everywhere you look in the Charleston Area. It rates just below

MUSC in patient satisfaction, however costs are consistently well above national average for almost every procedure category.

East Cooper Medical Center is a convenient general medical and surgical hospital in Mount Pleasant with 140 beds. It ranks below both MUSC and Roper-St. Francis hospitals in patient satisfaction and also charges more for procedures than the national average.

Trident Health comprises acute care hospitals—Trident Medical Center, Summerville Medical Center and Moncks Corner Medical Center. Trident gets satisfactory reviews from patients but charges more than the national average for procedures.

Finding a Doctor

There is an urgent care center on nearly every corner in the Charleston area. There are two MEDcare clinics, one in West Ashley and North Charleston, six CVS Minute Clinics, the well-respected Durst Family Medicine on Sullivan's Island, five Nason Medical Centers, Palmetto Primary Care Physicians Urgent Care, and many more.

Finding a new primary care doctor when you move to a new city can be difficult. Your best bet is to ask new friends and neighbors whom they recommend or use a site such as HealthGrades to research family practice providers as well as pediatricians and specialists.

There are nine community blood banks in the Charleston area; two are Red Cross centers and one is associated with Roper St. Francis. The Red Cross also has many mobile donations sites.

Veterans can find healthcare at the Ralph H. Johnson VA Medical Center in downtown Charleston. The hospital offers healthcare, a Veterans Crisis Line and PTSD treatment along with a comprehensive list of services for mental, health and holistic wellness services. Overall, it scored 80 out of 100 according to research firm FindTheBest. In the past the hospital struggled with long wait times for new patients (45 day average in 2014), but today their wait time has been dramatically reduced to a commendable average of 4 days.

There are over 30 hospice facilities in the area, including Hospice of Charleston, Heartland Hospice, and Gentiva Health Care.

CHAPTER 6

CHOOSING WHERE TO LIVE

The good news is Charleston is still affordable and buying a home here is a great investment. However, without doing a little homework, it can be confusing trying to figure out which neighborhood is best for you. Take time to make a strategy and you'll be able to relax and enjoy your house hunt. Here are five steps for finding the perfect Charleston home:

Step 1: Decide what you want. Make a list of what is most important to you in a home. Each person making the home-buying decision should answer for himself or herself so you both know what's important to the other. After you've made your list, rank how important each feature is to you. Decide what you have to have and where you can compromise. Once you've done this exercise, you'll be able to drastically narrow your search. Use this list of questions to help you and your family explore what's most important to each of you. Get the PDF version of this chart online: www.MovingtoCharlestonSCGuide.com.

Step 2: Decide on a budget. Your final number should include what you want to pay for monthly mortgage principle and interest, real estate taxes, mortgage insurance premiums (if applicable to you), homeowners insurance and neighborhood association fees. For each home you look at, ask your realtor to find out current figures on these costs.

Step 3: Get an idea of where you want to shop for homes: Read this book, highlight neighborhoods that sound interesting to you, and make notes for your realtor.

QUESTIO…					Ranking: Buyer #2
How far am … marina?					
How far ar…					
How far a… Charleston…					
How many bedrooms do I want?					
Do I need a yard?					
Do I want to be within walking distance to shopping and restaurants?					
Do I need a garage?					
Am I willing to do renovations?					
Are schools an important factor?					
Do I need boat storage or a dock?					
Would I consider building a new home?					
Is historic charm important?					
Does my neighborhood need good walking, biking or running paths?					
Townhome, condo or single-family home?					
Other #1:					
Other #2:					
Other #3:					
Other #4:					
Other #5:					

Step 4: Get a map: With 27 different cities and a warren of neighborhoods in each, deciphering our unique navigational jargon can make you crazy. You can download and print a map for free from the Charleston Area Visitor's Bureau website. Highlight Mark Clark Expressway, Highway 17, Highway 41, Interstate 26, the IOP Connector and other roads that come up in your real estate search. Note that I-526, the Mark Clark Expressway, makes a half circle around the area ending in Mount Pleasant to the east and West Ashley to the west. It's like a Pac Man eating the peninsula and James Island. Any property inside that half circle is "inside Mark Clark"

and everything else is "outside Mark Clark". What's the difference? Sometimes not much, but properties inside tend to be more desirable and some insurance rates depend on Mark Clark as a dividing line.

Step 5: Do some homework. Realtor.com has a fantastic app that allows you to draw a circle around an area and see all the homes that are for sale (and apartments for rent). It also has helpful sort features. If you need a realtor, the Charleston Trident Association of Realtors has a handy online search.

Neighborhoods

There are hundreds of different neighborhoods in the Charleston area. You may already feel overwhelmed if you've been trying to sort them out. Don't worry. You'll get a feel for the area quickly. You wouldn't want to read an exhaustive list of hundreds of neighborhood descriptions, so I've boiled the list down to popular and notable neighborhoods. If you start here you're likely to either find exactly what you're looking for, or it will lead you and your realtor to just the right neighborhood.

The features are based on popular items in a house hunt, plus a few more that might be important to you. For example, you may want to walk or bike to a grocery store and restaurants. If you also like to walk or run every morning, you probably want at least three miles of nice sidewalks or trails. If you think you'll find yourself downtown a few times a week, you won't want to be more than 10 miles away from East Bay Street. If you want to walk or bike to the beach, set a five-mile radius around the barrier islands. Then, of course, consider your budget.

Here's a list in graph form, plus a few other categories such as the ability to build a new home, historic value and access to deep water boat slips or a marina. Also included is an icon that indicates the neighborhood's public schools scored above average on GreatSchools. org.

LEGEND	
Price range	$ = Average / $$ - Above Average / $$$ Most Expensive
<5 miles to beach	⭐
Nice walking or jogging sidewalks or trails	👟
Easy walk or bike to shops and restaurants	☕
Historic	📷
Deep water dock or close to marina	⛵
<10 miles from downtown Charleston	🌉
Public schools ranked above average	🚶
New construction possible	**N**
Condos or Townhouses available	**C**

Historic Downtown

Downtown Charleston has 18 distinct neighborhoods. Prices start very high on the tip of the peninsula and gradually drop the further north you go. Kristin Walker, a local realtor with Dunes Properties, offers a detailed description of each of these distinct neighborhoods on her website, CharlestonInsideOut.net.

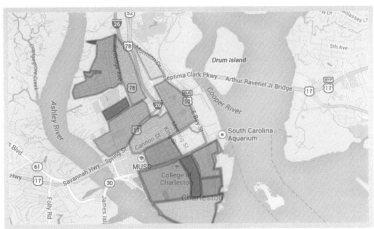

A map of downtown Charleston neighborhoods
Courtesy Realtor Kristin Walker & <u>CharlestonInsideOut.net</u>

MY NOTES:
NEIGHBORHOODS OF INTEREST TO SPEAK TO MY REALTOR ABOUT

Here's a look at features in the downtown neighborhoods:

NEIGHBORHOOD FEATURES		🥿	☕	📷	⛵	C
South of Broad	$$$	🥿	☕	📷	⛵	C
French Quarter	$$ - $$$	🥿	☕	📷		C
King Street - Historic	$$ - $$$	🥿	☕	📷		C
Ansonborough	$$ - $$$	🥿	☕	📷	⛵	
Harleston Village	$$ - $$$	🥿	☕	📷	⛵	
Mazyck-Wraggborough	$$ - $$$	🥿	☕	📷		
Cannonbourough	$ - $$$	🥿	☕	📷		
Radcliffbourough	$$$	🥿	☕	📷		C
Westside	$-$$$	🥿	☕	📷		C
Hampton Park Terrace	$-$$$	🥿	☕	📷		
North Central	$-$$$	🥿	☕	📷		
Wagener Terrace	$-$$	🥿	☕	📷		
NoMo	$$	🥿	☕			

Downtown Charleston

Notice there aren't any school, beach or new construction icons on this chart: Although the peninsula is surrounded by water, you'll have to travel at least 15 minutes from downtown to get to a beach. New construction isn't entirely out of the question but you'd be hard pressed to find a spot to build a house.

Finally, though most downtown schools don't rank above average, there are schools that rank at least average, and that's not bad. It doesn't mean you shouldn't send your kids to school downtown. Local officials have spent tens of millions of dollars renovating downtown elementary schools and they are truly beautiful works of art. And, teachers and administrators are working hard to bring up test scores so there's every reason to believe that the next few years will be a renaissance for downtown public schools. If you have kids and you want to live downtown, there's no reason you can't be part of the solution.

Mount Pleasant

Mount Pleasant is a wildly popular choice because there are so many options in so many price ranges—and you're rarely more than 15 minutes from a beach or downtown. This is a short list of the most popular or notable neighborhoods extracted from a list of more than 80 neighborhoods in Mount Pleasant; there are many more to choose from and you'll have fun discovering them as you shop.

It's hard to beat Seaside Farms for location and amenities. Just over the IOP Connector bridge, this neighborhood has a Target, a Harris Teeter, excellent cafes, pubs and restaurants, a hair and nail salon, a veterinarian and groomer, a yoga studio and a couple of clothing boutiques. There is also a nice hotel for overflow houseguests. Options in this neighborhood are single-family homes in the $500,000 + range, Long Grove condominiums from $100,000 to $250,000, Franke independent and assisted living houses and condos, and the unique Marais townhouse neighborhood in the $500,000 + range. Riviera at Seaside has several new apartments and townhomes for rent.

Watermark is a planned community that offers Lowcountry homes with all the modern amenities. You can buy an existing home or build your own gorgeous single family home for around $600,000 to $700,000. Watermark also has an apartment and condo community.

Old Village Mount Pleasant is a quaint, historic neighborhood that faces the Charleston Peninsula. Homes are grand, expansive, and highly sought after. If you can afford the million-dollar price tag, this is a fantastic walking neighborhood with a few shops and excellent restaurants.

NEIGHBORHOOD FEATURES

Mount Pleasant	Price	★	👞	☕	🌉	🧍	📷	⛵	C	N
Seaside Farms	$$	★	👞	☕	🌉	🧍			C	
Watermark	$$		👞		🌉	🧍			C	N
Old Village	$$$	★	👞	☕	🌉	🧍	📷			
Dunes West	$$		👞			🧍			C	N
Park West	$$		👞	☕		🧍		⛵	C	N
Hamlin Plantation	$$		👞			🧍			C	N
Rivertowne	$$					🧍		⛵	C	N
I'On	$$$		👞	☕	🌉	🧍			C	
Belle Hall	$		👞	☕	🌉	🧍			C	N
Simmons Point	$$	★		☕	🌉	🧍			C	
Marsh Harbor	$$	★			🌉	🧍		⛵	C	
The Tides	$$$		👞	☕	🌉	🧍			C	
The Renaissance	$$$		👞		🌉	🧍			C	

Dunes West, Park West, Hamlin Plantation, Carolina Park, and Rivertowne are a few of several planned communities in Mount Pleasant where you can buy or build a home. If you don't mind being a little farther from the beach and downtown, these are beautiful, quiet communities with prices in the $250,000s to $1,000,000.

I'On Village is a unique planned community that you must see to believe. Architectural styles range from Gothic to Italianate to Modern Lowcountry. Prices start in the $600,000s and run into the millions. This breathtaking neighborhood has a country club, shops, and restaurants and is minutes from downtown. Do yourself a favor and at least stop by their Irish pub for lunch and a walk.

Belle Hall may be Mount Pleasant's best buy. Single-family homes and condos in this neighborhood can still be had in the $200,000 range, and you're just across the street from all the restaurants and shopping you want. It doesn't hurt that you're also fairly close to the beach and downtown.

Simmon's Point and Marsh Harbor are small, unique condo and townhouse neighborhoods on Ben Sawyer Boulevard just across from Sullivan's Island. Marsh Harbor features deep-water docks, expansive water views and lovely architecture. Simmon's Point has older architecture and smaller footprints—but still offers stunning views of the marsh and the intercostal waterway. Prices range from $400,000 to $1,000,000.

No description of Mount Pleasant housing would be complete without including two iconic condo buildings: The Tides and The Renaissance. These complexes are on either side of the ramp to the Ravenel Bridge—The Tides to the north and The Renaissance to the south on the Patriot's Point side. Both have panoramic views of the bridge, the river and cargo ship traffic. Prices range in the $800,000s to $2,000,000.

The Barrier Islands

Daniel Island, Sullivan's Island, Isle of Palms, James Island, John's Island and Folly Beach are the most popular island choices in the area.

Daniel Island is the only one of the group that is not a barrier island. There's a lot to love here, plus great schools, but it lacks a beach. Isle of Palms and Sullivan's Island are the perfect choice for sand lovers who can afford island living. James and John's Island are large and diverse and have excellent options. Folly Beach is a laid-back island reminiscent of Key West before The Gap invaded Duval Street. On Folly, school choices aren't as good as Mount Pleasant or West Ashley, but they are at least average and there are private school choices.

NEIGHBORHOOD FEATURES										
Daniel Island	$-$$$		👞	☕	🌉	🚶		⛵	C	N
Isle of Palms	$$$	⭐	👞	☕		🚶		⛵	C	N
Sullivan's Island	$$$	⭐	👞	☕	🌉	🚶	📷	⛵	C	N
James Island	$		👞		🌉	🚶		⛵	C	N
Folly Beach	$-$$$	⭐	👞	☕	🌉			⛵	C	N
John's Island	$-$$$		👞						C	N

(row label: The Islands)

West Ashley

West Ashley, so named because it's west of the Ashley River, is one of Charleston's oldest residential neighborhoods. Parts of the area are scenic with mature trees, water views and majestic estate homes, and parts are home to big box stores and malls. The convenience factor is so high that no matter where in Charleston you choose to live, you will find yourself running errands in West Ashley at some point. From 1950's starter homes to older bungalow renovation opportunities to stately homes with deep-water docks; West Ashley has homes in all price ranges. Living here puts you within minutes of downtown Charleston. Many of the hospitals' medical employees live in West Ashley and bike across the bridge to work. You'll have a pleasant 15 or 20 minute drive to nearby Folly Beach.

NEIGHBORHOOD FEATURES								
The Crescent	$$$	👟	☕	🌉	🚶	⛵		
Byrnes Down	$-$$	👟	☕	🌉	🚶			
Windermere	$-$$	👟	☕	🌉	🚶	⛵		
Wappoo Heights	$$$	👟	☕	🌉	🚶	⛵		
Avondale	$-$$	👟	☕	🌉	🚶	⛵		
Carolina Bay	$-$$	👟		🌉	🚶		C	N

West Ashley

Housing choices

Charleston probably has more types of housing available than most cities of its size. Truly creative options abound! How about living in a cozy, historic carriage house? The weather is mild in the winter—how about living on a boat full time? Restored historic mansions are in good supply, as are historic fixer-uppers if you want to get your hands dirty. If you're ready to build your dream house, empty lots and land are plentiful.

Quaint craftsman cottages abound, as do luxury townhouses and condominiums. If you care more about having fun outside, you can easily find an inexpensive, basic townhouse or condo within walking or biking distance of a beach. If you've always wanted to live in a historic mansion or building but you can't swing the monthly payment, you can buy into part of one and enjoy the perks without the price tag. All of these options are sprinkled all over the Charleston area, so it's worthwhile to engage a good real estate agent who has a long history in Charleston.

State of the Real Estate Market

Charleston's real estate market peaked in 2007 then took a dive— along with almost every other city in the nation. It's interesting to note that Charleston's real estate low point was only 12.9% below the peak—not too bad considering how other regions' prices collapsed. According to the Charleston Trident Association of Realtors (CTAR), recovery began slowly in 2010 with sales up 3% from 2009. Sales were wobbly in 2011 with activity dropping 2.7% from 2010. Things began to look up in 2012, but 2013 was the real benchmark for recovery with sales up 8.7% over the year before. In 2014 the market rose 8% over 2013, 2015 rose 6.5% over 2014, and 2016 is showing 6% increases over 2015.

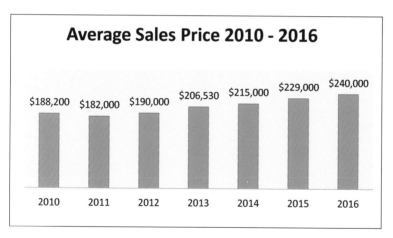

Word is out that Charleston is an incredible place to call home. No matter where you choose to live, now is an excellent time to invest in Charleston real estate.

Real Estate Services

Having a good real estate agent along for your Charleston home search is essential, and there are several agencies from which to choose. If you have it narrowed down, it's a good idea to choose a realtor that specializes in your area.

Renting vs. Buying

Should you rent or buy when first moving here? It's a great idea to rent, at least for a few months so you can get the feel of the islands and our many diverse neighborhoods. Renting allows you to see which areas best suit your new life. On the other hand, rentals aren't as common as they are in other cities, so you may not have a lot of choices. Just know that it's hard to make a mistake when choosing an area of Charleston —they all have their unique charm. Home prices will likely continue to increase, so if you've got your down payment ready, dive right in!

CHAPTER 7

SHOPPING

If you're used to mega malls, unlimited options and shopping like it's an Olympic sport, Charleston may be an adjustment for you. Life is just simpler in the Lowcountry and we tend have smaller wardrobes, functional furniture and housewares and less stuff in general. That's not to say there isn't great shopping in Charleston, but it can be spread out.

Charleston has a style all it's own, due to the climate and beloved traditions, so most locals are only mildly interested in what people are wearing in New York or Milan. When it comes to style, most store buyers bring home only those trends that will work in Charleston. That makes for small shops with carefully curated selections. The selection may be more limited than bigger cities, but the quality of the selection is far better (and not necessarily more expensive). Also, clothiers in Charleston love to help transplants understand Charleston style. Don't be shy when you shop, ask for help and you'll get the perfect outfit for the occasion and some new local friends.

There's more to Charleston fashion than dresses and cabana shirts. For couture style, both locals and well-informed visitors make a stop at Gwynn's of Mount Pleasant to browse international runway trends that will work in Charleston and beyond. (Owner Marshall Simon even posts his cell phone number right on the website in case you ever have a fashion emergency. People use it.) In Old Town Mount Pleasant, staff at the Out of Hand boutique can help you master the art of Charleston fashion—with your own personal flair. If you want to dress like a local, just wander downtown's historic King Street and replace your wardrobe of all-black synthetics with colorful cotton and linen. While you're at it, you can replace those towering stilettos with cobblestone-friendly wedges. You can also swap your collection of navy blue power ties and white shirts with funky bowties and cool pastel shirts.

Life's little luxuries can be found on King Street
Photo courtesy Jason Crichton Photography

When it comes to furniture and home goods, the climate and lifestyle figure in heavily as well: Everything has to stand up to humidity, heat, houseguests, sand, and the salty air. Basic linens from Target or HomeGoods can take frequent laundering and furniture is never so precious that kids, guests, and dogs are discouraged from post-beach naps on the sofa.

Grocery and Gourmet Items

If you're a gourmet cook, grocery shopping may require an adjustment as well. Charleston is a real foodie town so we definitely have our share of gourmet shops. But, like everything else, they're a bit spread out. Local foodies start Saturday mornings at the Farmer's Market in Marion Square where they fill up canvas bags with whatever local fruits and vegetables are in season. They'll also pick up fresh local eggs, meat, shrimp, handmade pasta and baguettes from the same vendors week after week.

Get your fresh pasta from Rio Bertolini at the Mount Pleasant or downtown Farmer's Market

Then, there may be a stop at the cheese shop for hors d'oeuvre and wine. If fish is on that evening's menu, you can stop at a seafood counter—likely right on a dock close to home. It's also not unusual to send part of the household crew out fishing, shrimping or crabbing for that evening's entrée. Of course, if you're looking for one-stop shopping, you will find an abundance of Harris-Teeter and BI-LO grocery stores, a Whole Foods and a Trader Joe's in Mount Pleasant, and an Earth Fare on James Island

Make a stop in the Seaside Farms neighborhood at The Crescent Olive for their delightful oil and balsamic vinegar tasting tours. Then pop into Saveurs Du Monde, a few doors down for authentic French pastries made by a real French pastry chef. While you're in the neighborhood, Ardoa Wine Bar around the corner offers a wonderfully curated selection of wines from around the world. Locals get the daily catch right off the dock at Mount Pleasant Seafood on Shem Creek. Downtown, stop by goat. sheep. cow for an excellent selection of cheese and wine.

Tasting before buying is encouraged at friendly goat.sheep.cow
Photo Courtesy goat.sheep.cow

Just a block down from the cheese shop you can buy fresh bread from Normandy Farm. You can get your French pastry and macaroon fix downtown either at the Macaroon Café on John Street or at Christophe, which is tucked away on Society Street. Christophe also has a small selection of excellent sandwiches on fresh baguettes that make a perfect quick lunch or beach picnic. Beer lovers adore Charleston because it's easy to get a growler of local brew almost anywhere—even Whole Foods has a filling station. Be sure to check out the Charleston Beer Exchange downtown for the best selection of local and international brews anywhere in the city.

Also downtown, Caviar & Bananas has a carefully chosen selection of gourmet items, as does Bull Street Market. On Sullivan's Island, stop by The Co-Op, a tiny but wonderful one-stop shop for gourmet lunch or dinner. In West Ashley, you can check out Avondale Wine & Cheese where the owners are passionate about helping you find the right pairings.

The Unique Charleston Kitchen

Charleston kitchens have long revolved around local dishes, lively cocktail parties, and large family dinners. As a result, you'll find some unique and important serving ware in a Lowcountry pantry. For example, Charleston Rice Spoons are large, long-handled spoons traditionally used to serve rice at Sunday suppers. They make wonderful hostess gifts, and you can find them at local boutiques such as Croghan's Jewel Box and Viewtemps on King Street. You may also want to choose several oyster plates for serving oysters on the half shell, a staple appetizer at cocktail parties. While you can buy new oyster plates, scouring King Street antiques shops for a vintage plate is a lovely way to spend an afternoon. Speaking of cocktail parties, if you've ever wanted to outfit a sparkling, welcoming bar or bar cart – your move to Charleston is the perfect opportunity. The cocktail hour is alive and well in the Holy City, so invest in a nice set of highball glasses, wine glasses and champagne flutes and you'll be ready to welcome new friends in true Charleston style.

All-Inclusive Shopping Centers

If you need chain-store retail therapy, head to Mount Pleasant's Towne Center mall where you'll find Barnes & Noble, Bed, Bath & Beyond, Ann Taylor, Bath & Body Works, The Gap, Chico's, J. Jill, GNC and most of the other usual suspects. Towne Center also has hair and nail salons, Hairy Winston, a gourmet pet supply store, a sparkling movie theater, a Verizon, and a Lowes among many other standard retailers.

West Ashley has the Citadel Mall with even more national retailers, including Express, Foot Locker, Charlotte Russe, Men's Warehouse, and New York & Co. Nearby there's an enormous movie theater, a Target, Dick's Sporting Goods, World Market and just about every other store familiar to mall neighborhoods. If you can't find what you need in West Ashley's shopping district, you probably don't need it.

Tanger Outlets in North Charleston is an excellent place to get deep discounts on name brand clothes and accessories from Ralph Lauren, Coach, Saks Fifth Avenue, Kenneth Cole and more.

Department stores

Occasionally only a department store will do for the basics. Belk is the go-to in Mount Pleasant, while the nearby Marshall's and T.J. Maxx offer discounted prices on furniture, accessories and clothes for the whole family. In West Ashley you'll find Dillard's, J.C. Penny and Sears stores.

Shopping areas

Shopping downtown is mostly confined to historic King Street, although it's worth taking a detour to visit local favorite Indigo just off of Waterfront Park to shop for gifts, unique clothing, jewelry, Lowcountry-themed art and more.

**Indigo is Charleston's go-to stop for gifts,
local art and unique clothing and accessories**

Mount Pleasant has a variety of shops and boutiques spread through town, plus the Town Center mall. West Ashley is a shopper's mecca, but shopping on the islands is confined to beach gear stores or one or two clothing boutiques. On John's Island, Freshfields Village in Kiawah is a fantastic place to boost your coastal wardrobe.

Furniture & Design

If you want a mega furniture store with all the traditional offerings, you'll find a Haverty's and Rooms To Go in North Charleston. Downtown, you'll find a Pottery Barn and enjoy wandering through Morris Sokol on upper King Street. This gigantic furniture store started in Charleston in 1921 and has been family owned ever since. In Mount Pleasant and on Kiawah, you'll find a GDC Home with a nice range of coastal furnishings and free in-store design services (in-home is a modest fee). If you have more eclectic tastes, or if you just want to have some fun browsing, visit Celadon in Mount Pleasant or their warehouse outlet in North Charleston. This inspiring housewares and furniture store not only has unique items and free design services, it also welcomes pets and their people with beverages—now that's true southern hospitality!

**Celadon is great place to find ecclectic textiles,
furniture and home accessories
Photo courtesy Celadon**

Mount Pleasant is also home to the only Steven Shell retail store in the world. If your decorating tastes are bold or if you need a splash of color in all those coastal neutrals, this is where you'll find the perfect piece. *(Steven Shell furniture is only available through very select retailers, so the chance to browse an entire store full of this funky, eco-friendly, hard-to-get furniture is a real treat!)*

Dressing for the South Carolina Lifestyle

Take a walk downtown and you'll quickly get a handle on local style. Here, girls get to be girly in flowy skirts, bright dresses, and natural fibers. Savvy Chucktown chicks ditch the stilettos in favor of sandals, wedges, or flats. Watch a few visitors in Manolos pick their way down uneven sidewalks and cobblestones at a snail's pace and you'll quickly see why! Also absent are tight, flashy, revealing clothes, dark colors, enormous designer bags and obvious displays of affluence. Charleston women are understated, elegant, colorful, sporty, feminine, and natural.

Too often the guys are consigned to a drab fashion palette and limited choices. In Charleston fellows get to go tastefully wild. You'll need a Seersucker or linen suit, a few colorful bowties with coordinating linen or cotton shirts, and at least one pair of shoes with real personality. The best part? You get to sport a dashing hat on any occasion. Charleston style isn't splashy, preppy Nantucket style—it's more refined with a hint of confident mischief. Get some help from Ben Silver or Berlin's downtown and you'll be irresistible.

Want to dress like a local?
Shop Charleston's boutiques.

Andrea Serrano's blog, Charleston Shop Currator, can help you create your own unique Charleston style. (Photo courtesy Andrea Serrano.)

Charleston has recently gone through a style revitalization. The once popular uniform of seersucker suits and Lily Pulitzer prints, have been augmented by a more progressive approach to fashion. Charleston has emerged as a cosmopolitan destination for style in the south thanks to the booming economy and the community's support of local shops and brands.

Charleston's historic King Street has a legacy of locally owned boutiques that have spanned over 100 years. In the past 15 years numerous chain stores have been popping up and down the strip, capitalizing on this shopping mecca. Still, it's the local stores that really stand out, offering everything from upscale high-end designers to urban sleek sneakers. Charleston's shopping is a gem and probably boasts the most locally owned businesses in the south. With countless stores located in every neighborhood you can imagine from downtown, to Mt. Pleasant, Daniel Island, Sullivan's Island, West Ashley, Kiawah, James Island, and Folly Beach, the possibilities are infinite.

Andrea Serrano is a freelance fashion stylist, blogger, and TV host of Fashion Friday on Lowcountry Live on Channel 4 in Charleston. Her blog Charleston Shop Curator showcases the diversity of styles in the Lowcountry and is a great place to start learning about local fashion and where to find it.

CHAPTER 8

NEVER A SHORTAGE OF THINGS TO DO

Charleston's legendary social scene, outdoor activities, festivals and excellent weather means that there's always something fun going on.

Whether it's an oyster roast under the oaks, a winter bonfire on the beach, live music at the Pour House or Friday Night Art Walks downtown—you'll never be bored here.

Literary Arts

Blue Bicycle Books is the epicenter of Charleston's literary arts scene. Not only will you find an excellent selection of used, rare and local books here, you'll get connected with some of the most exciting events on Charleston's art's calendar. YALLfest, sponsored by Blue Bicycle and Amazon, is Charleston's annual Young Adult Book Festival where you can meet dozens of best-selling authors and sit in on panel discussions. The bookstore also hosts the annual Write of Summer creative writing camp for kids, fun book signings and many other literary events throughout the year. Plug into people and events at Blue Bicycle and you'll be plugged into intelligent, creative Charleston.

Blue Bicycle Books is the epicenter of Charleston's Literary Art scene.
Courtesy Blue Bicycle Books

Visual Arts

Charleston is well known as an art-lover's paradise. The best place to begin is on a Friday night art walk down Broad Street's Gallery Row, then stroll the galleries of the French Quarter and the Upper King Design District. On art walk nights, you'll be treated to wine and snacks while you browse. Don't miss fun opening nights at Robert Lange Studios, always voted the best gallery in Charleston. Meet emerging artists at The Art Mecca of Charleston. And, see inspiring exhibits at the innovative Redux Contemporary Art Center. Art lovers won't want to miss the Gibbes Museum of Art and the nearby Halsey Institute of Contemporary Art.

Art patrons enjoy the opening of
Reorientation at the Redux Contemporary Art Center
Photo courtesty Redux Contemporary Art Center

Performing Arts

For performing arts, check out a show at one of the area's many theaters, including the historic Sottile Theater, Dock Street Theater, and the Queen Street Playhouse. The Charleston Ballet Theater will charm you, as will the talented Charleston Symphony Orchestra.

Music

How Loud Is the Lowcountry? Charleston's Rich Music Scene

Photo courtesy Kris Manning

Charleston attracts thousands of travelers every year who are hungry for its culinary creativity, and the Holy City doesn't disappoint. But after dinner, many will find Charleston and its surrounding communities also offer a feast for the ears. On any given night, live music is just a step away—from the Peninsula, West Ashley and Folly Beach, to Mount Pleasant, Sullivan's Island and IOP. The local music scene in Charleston really rocks.

If you're in the mood for live and local music—whether it's singers and songwriters playing original tunes or an up-and-coming band—chances are, Monday through Sunday (yes, that's seven days a week), you won't be disappointed. Younger crowds may gravitate towards The Pour House, with its standing-room live club feel, while "post-college" professionals may seek out some of Charleston's more intimate venues, like The Sparrow in North Charleston's Park Circle neighborhood.

Turning it up a notch, national acts regularly roll through Charleston, performing at the Music Farm downtown and at the North Charleston Coliseum and Performing Arts Center. Annually, Charleston hosts the Spoleto and Piccolo Spoleto Festivals, which typically kick off Memorial Day weekend and wrap up in mid-June. These festivals attract some of the world's most talented performers in music, theater, art and dance. Seeing a Spoleto performance can inspire chills on a hot evening in the Lowcountry.

If jazz is more your style, you can just book a table at Charleston Grill in the Belmond Hotel (formerly Charleston Place). Nightly, Charleston Grill serves up some of the best live jazz in the South. Rumor has it jazz music traces its roots to Charleston, not New Orleans, as many believe. Why not ask one of the talented musicians there what she believes while you drop a tip in the jar?

**Kris Manning, That Drummer Girl
and Co-founder of The Music Battery**

Historic Sites

Charleston is so infused with history that you can spend a lifetime here and never quite get around to seeing all the sights. One of the best places to start getting acquainted with the history of your new hometown is the Preservation Society of Charleston at the corner of King and Queen Streets. History lovers will find books on every subject relevant to Charleston's history. Pick up one or two of the self-guided walk brochures and spend a leisurely afternoon poking around the nooks and crannies of Charleston's historic sites.

Get a ticket for Charleston's Museum Mile and you can meander up the one-mile section of Meeting Street visiting six museums, five beautiful historic homes, four parks, the Revolutionary War powder magazine, and the many historic churches and public buildings that are of national importance. The Charleston Museum has such an interesting array of local artifacts that even non-museum lovers will be engrossed. It's estimated that nearly half of the slaves that entered the country entered through Charleston's ports and The Old Slave Mart Museum is a must-see for those interested in African-American history. Of course, there are so many historic sites relevant to the Revolutionary and Civil wars that it will take you a few wonderful years to take them in. A good start is Fort Sumter in the Charleston harbor and Fort Moultrie on Sullivan's Island.

Gullah Geechie

The Gullah Geechie Cultural Heritage Corridor runs through Charleston. This beloved culture is part of daily life in Charleston. Gullah Geechie is a fusion of African and European language, stories, food, crafts and history—and Charleston embraces and protects these disappearing traditions. It won't be long before you incorporate at least a few Gullah Geechie words in your vocabulary, and more than one recipe will find it's way into your list of favorites.

Spoleto and Piccolo Spoleto

Of course, Charleston's biggest cultural extravaganza is the annual Spoleto Festival and Piccolo Spoleto Festival. For 17 nights every June visitors from all over the world join locals for diverse, world-class visual, literary, music, dance, and theater events. Locals get discount tickets and there are many free events.

Gastronomic Delights

If you love good food, you're going to love living in Charleston. From James Beard award-winning chefs, to traditional Gullah cuisine, to friends throwing a good Lowcountry boil, Charleston has a mind-bending array of food options.

You'll find plenty of excellent local seafood on every menu, along with a healthy helping of biscuits and grits on the side. But, Charleston's chefs don't stop at traditional fare. And, it's actually difficult to find a restaurant that doesn't feature local ingredients and a farm-to-table attitude. From Southern fried comfort food to health and eco-conscious cuisine, Charleston has it all.

Edmund's Oast has been called one of the best restaurants in the South
Photo courtesty Chrys Rynearson

Eating is a social activity here, so plan to ramp up your restaurant budget. You might want to adopt the local habit of spending Saturday mornings getting in a fun outdoor workout by surfing, paddleboarding, walking the four-mile Ravenel bridge or jogging The Battery in anticipation of that evening's feast—or a big Sunday morning brunch with friends.

How to pick a good restaurant? Ask a local, especially a bartender or the wait staff wherever you're lunching. Downtown, local favorites include cozy, quaint Chez Nous for French, Spanish and Northern Italian cuisine and Southern hospitality; The Grocery where the menu consists almost entirely of local ingredients; Circa 1886—Charleston's most romantic restaurant; Bin 152 for the best cheese, charcuterie and wine in town, and The Macintosh for a modern spin on traditional Southern cuisine. Edmund's Oast, with it's 40 craft brews on tap, is being called "the best new restaurant in the South", and nearby Indaco is the perfect place to satisfy your craving for real Italian food. You won't go wrong with any restaurant on East Bay Street, but venture out to the neighborhoods for tucked away gems like Trattoria Lucca. You'll have to circle the block for parking, but it's worth it.

**Indaco on Upper King Street is a great spot for rustic Italian food.
Photo courtesy Andrew Cebulka**

If you're at the Isle of Palms or Sullivan's Island beach, Middle Street on Sullivan's Island has a nice selection of casual restaurants. You'll find a good burger at Poe's, excellent modern tacos at Mex 1 and traditional Irish pub grub and live music at Dunlevy's. Tucked away further down Middle Street is The Obstinate Daughter, an interesting mix of raw bar and Italian cuisine. For a quick beach lunch, stop in The Co-Op for to-go sandwiches, snacks, and packaged homemade dinners.

Night Life

Speaking of late nights, there's one thing Charleston isn't—an all-hours party town. You won't find the loud, tipsy crowds you'll find in Daytona Beach or Key West. Charlestonians don't guzzle daiquiris from a bucket or drink beer from glass boots. Instead, if we're up late you'll find us enjoying old-fashioned cocktails at The Gin Joint or listening to jazz at The Mezz above Sermet's on King Street. Summer nights we gather on the Stars Rooftop for drinks with 360-degree views of the city. Or, if it's really late, we join a throng of just-off-work servers and bartenders for a 3 a.m. nosh at <u>Butcher & Bee</u>. For music, we head to <u>The Pour House</u>, a late-night tradition on James Island.

**Charleston has some of the best cuisine in the world
and it's not all shrimp and grits**

Sports

Charleston is a golfer's paradise. With <u>nineteen scenic courses around the area</u>, you can work on your swing year-round. Kiawah has some of the most beautiful courses in the country. Their links regularly attract A-list celebrities and world leaders trying to relax—or broker big deals. Many neighborhood golf courses have reasonable fees and memberships.

Tennis

Tennis lovers: Get excited. *Tennis Magazine* named Charleston "America's Best Tennis Town" 11 years in a row. The Family Circle Tennis Center on Daniel Island is home to the Volvo Car Open. Every Spring you can watch tennis greats like Serena and Venus Williams battle it out with other tennis legends like Andrea Petkovic and Caroline Wozniacki. Wild Dunes resort has 17 Har-Tru courts and Kiawah Island Tennis Resort has nine. Membership-based courts include Charleston Tennis Center, Maybank Tennis Center and the Family Circle Tennis Center. There are 13 free public courts in the Charleston area.

Parks

Charleston is understandably proud of its national and county parks—many are like nothing else in the world. Want to camp or rent a costal cabin, catch your own crabs for dinner, kayak or bike some of the most beautiful trails in the Lowcountry? Visit the James Island County Park. Want to learn to kayak, paddleboard, ride a zip line or climb a rock wall? There's a program for that. You can rent boats, bikes, kayaks, and paddleboards at many parks. Or, you can take a break from the sand and salt at the Splash Park. There are several off-leash dog parks in the area as well as public docks for fishing, crabbing and launching boats.

If you love wildlife, the Cape Romaine National Wildlife Refuge will be your favorite weekend getaway. Cape Romaine is a 22-mile segment of the Atlantic coast set aside for conservation. You can visit on your own or via guided tours year round. Before you go, pick up a copy of Exploring Bull Island: Sailing and Walking Around a South Carolina Sea Island by Bob Raynor. You'll learn about the history of the area, including who's buried on the island and the indigenous people who once called it home, as well as how to navigate the alligators, snakes and insects that are now the island's only tenants.

Great blue herons are frequent visitors to marshes and ponds.
Photo courtesy Jason Crichton Photography

Fitness

How do locals eat all those biscuits and drink all those Bloody Marys and stay so fit? By taking exercise not-so-seriously. That's right, if we have to exercise, we prefer to have fun. There are a few great gyms spread around but most people stay fit by taking it outside and making it social. Nearly half of Charleston households have at least one dog, and those morning dog walks are a popular way to stay fit and meet up with friends. Of course, water sports burn serious calories while building strength—and you can paddleboard, hike, sail, kayak and surf year-round. Yoga here is down-to-earth and popular with all ages and abilities. You'll find friendly classes in nearly every neighborhood. Walkers and runners stay fit training for the annual Cooper River Bridge Run or just by taking in the sea breezes on the beach or the Ravenel Bridge.

Charleston is a fit town and the social nature of many physical activities will add a lot of motivation to your fitness commitment.

Boating

If you have a boat or want a boat, public landings are plentiful. Boaters spend easy days, nights and weekends cruising the harbor, the creeks or the coast in search of fish—or just peace and quiet. Sailing is a popular pastime (and competitive sport) in Charleston. In fact, Charleston is the home of the largest keelboat regatta in North America. Every year hundreds of sailors from all over the world converge on the harbor and just offshore for Charleston Race Week. Even if you're a landlubber, it's fun to watch from shore. Competitive types can join the Charleston Ocean Racing Association (CORA) and race their sailboats (or crew on someone else's) in the harbor and offshore races. If you've always wanted to learn to sail, the College of Charleston offers private lessons, as does the Charleston Sailing School. Retired sailing instructor Captain John Springer also conducts private 'Learn to Sail' days or weekends aboard his sturdy 30' Morgan sailboat, Direction. There are several yacht clubs and many marinas in the area, most of them full of friendly people.

Fishing Charters

Not only can you catch amazing fish on a Charleston fishing charter, many captains know which restaurants will cook them up for you! Check out The Reel Deal, Yates Sea Charters or Charleston Sport Fishing. Expect to catch red and black drum, spotted sea trout, grouper, flounder, jack, mackerel and much more.

Sunset Cruises

You absolutely must see the Charleston skyline from the water, and you must do it as soon as possible. Several local captains offer the opportunity for private harbor sails including Captain John Springer aboard Direction, Captain Dustin Kent aboard Fate and Captain Banff Luther aboard his lovely catamaran Om.

Sail the harbor and you're likely to spot dolphins and diving birds before the sun slips behind the steeples of the Holy City. Want to take a turn at the helm or join in a Wednesday night race? No problem. Want to propose or celebrate a special occasion? Local captains can hook you up.

**Guests aboard the sailing yacht _Fate_ enjoy
a golden sunset over the Holy City
Photo courtesy Dustin K. Ryan Photography**

If you've always wanted to sail a tall ship, or aren't so sure about being out on the water, *The Schooner Pride* is a great way to see Charleston at sunset. The Pride is an 84-foot Tall Ship that takes larger groups out for two-hour harbor sails. The small crew is friendly and knowledgeable and goes out of their way to make sure everyone is comfortable. Beverages are sold onboard (by law you can't bring your own) but it's okay to bring your own snacks.

For a sunset with a party atmosphere, board the *Palmetto Breeze* from the Shem Creek dock in front of Red's Ice House. The Breeze is a gigantic, stable catamaran with a barefoot bar and plenty of fun to go around. Water and soda are free and there is a full cash bar.

Watercraft Rentals

Tidal Wave Water Sports rents power boats and wave runners if you want to tool around the Isle of Palms, or try Charleston Power Boat Rental if you'd like to shove off from the city marina downtown. If you have an ASA certification and you'd like to rent a sailboat, Charleston Sailing School rents four sizes of sailing yachts for bareboat charters.

Kayak and paddleboard rentals are plentiful, especially along Shem Creek, a popular place to spot dolphins and birds. Try Nature Adventure Outfitters and Charleston Outdoor Adventures on the same side of the creek as Red's Icehouse. Coastal Expeditions rents on Shem Creek, Folly Beach and Isle of Palms and they also offer excellent guided expeditions off the beaten path. Taking a trip with Coastal Expeditions is a good way to learn to sea kayak and safety on the ocean and in the marshes before setting out on your own. Once you're ready to take off by yourself, you can rent a variety of kayaks, including tandems, fishing and peddle-drive kayaks from Time Out Sports in Mount Pleasant. The friendly staff will loan you foam blocks, help you load your boat and, if you buy a kayak from them, they'll take off the price of your rental. While you're at Time Out, pick up a copy of Kayak Charleston, a true labor of love by Ralph Earhart. This is the local kayaking bible and an absolute must-have for kayakers.

Birding

Charleston has a fascinating year-round population of birds, and is an important migration stop for a variety of ducks, storks and warblers. The result is an ever-changing show that will delight even beginning birders. Cape Romaine is the place to spot birds you never thought you'd see, including swallowtail kites, the elusive black crowned night heron and roseate spoonbills. Painted buntings favor Folly Beach and all manner of diving ducks overwinter in Mount Pleasant's many small lakes. Of course, the marshes are filled with feathered wonders including wood storks, ibis and herons of all sizes and colors. Even non-birders will enjoy The Center for Birds of Prey, situated on 152-acres, this incredible facility is home to activities for research, education and avian welfare. They also have a medical clinic that treats more than 500 injured birds of prey each year. (If you find an injured bird, call the center right away.)

Hiking

You'll see stickers on local cars proclaiming, "I climbed Mount Pleasant". That's an inside joke that refers to "hiking" across the Ravenel Bridge, half of which is in Mount Pleasant and the other half in Charleston. Hiking in the Lowcountry may not rival hiking out West, but there are plenty of opportunities for a good walk in nature. Start with the trails in Francis Marion and Sumter National Forests, then take the Bull Island Ferry out to hike Bull Island and the Cape Romaine National Wildlife Refuge, which includes one of Charleston's famous "boneyard beaches". You can also hike and camp on uninhabited Capers Island with a permit. Hiking in the Lowcountry requires some special precautions. Bring more water and sun protection than you think you'll need and be prepared to encounter alligators, venomous snakes and plenty of mosquitos. If you don't disturb them, they usually won't disturb you. Walk mindfully and you'll easily be able to share the land with Charleston's more notorious wild critters.

Insider's Tip: Free Beach Gear

If you're trying to build a stash of beach gear, take a walk on the beach early Saturday and Sunday evenings. Many visitors who have to fly home leave brand new chairs, umbrellas, skim boards and coolers propped against the yellow trash cans in hopes they'll find a good home.

Bicycle Tours

Charleston is flat as a pancake. Unless you have to go up and over a bridge, bicycling here is easy. There are several bike tour companies that offer guided and self-service tours. Try Charleston Bicycle Tours for a full vacation experience, or rent a bike from The Bicycle Shoppe or Affordabike downtown and take off for one of the many county parks.

CHAPTER 9
FROM PRE-K TO POST GRAD

Raising kids in Charleston is a great experience. Because we live in rhythm with the natural world here, children develop an early appreciation for ecology and the wonders of nature. Of course, learning to swim, surf, fish, and sail is more fun when you're young. The wide variety of outdoor entertainment keeps young ones active and healthy. After all, who wants to play video games when there are sandcastles to build?

Moreover, schools tend to be very good in the Charleston area, with just a few exceptions. All Charleston schools have initiatives aimed at improving literacy, student performance, teacher education, parent involvement and environmental health and sustainability. Charleston is also home to excellent colleges and continuing education opportunities.

Infant & Toddler Care

There are hundreds of choices for childcare in Charleston ranging from private, in-home care to faith-based and Montessori programs. ChildcareCenter.us maintains a list of safe, quality childcare organizations in the tri-county area along with a description of their mission statement and programs offered. State mandates a staff-to-child ratio of no more than 1:5, and the young population is growing and creating more demand for daycare. So, it's a good idea to research early because you may face waiting lists. The average cost of childcare in Charleston is $150 – $200 per week.

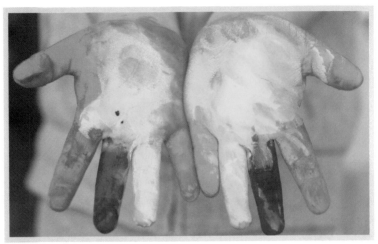

Charleston has many opportunities for creative education

Public & Private Schools

All parents want their children to have access to the best education possible. But, moving to a new city and choosing a neighborhood with a good school can be overwhelming. In Charleston, it's fairly simple: Our schools rank very high against the national average; of nearly 200 schools only five are at-risk. Thus, most neighborhoods will also come with great education opportunities for your kids.

Ninety percent of Charleston's kids attend one of 130 public schools. Public school choices include Charter, Magnet and Independent schools—some of which are award winning.

High school students must have 24 credits in diverse subjects, including computer science, foreign language or career and technology. They must pass an English and Math assessment in order to graduate. There are 45 private schools in the area and all have a religious affiliation. You can find a list and description of each on the Private School Review.

Overall, Charleston area schools are excellent with scores above the national average. The chart below shows area schools with a GreatSchools ranking 8 or higher out of a perfect 10. Note that not all schools are ranked by GreatSchools so there may be more options in your area

SCHOOL	LOCATION	GREATSCHOOLS RANKING
Stiles Point Elementary School	James Island	9
Fort Johnson Middle School	James Island	9
James Island Charter High School	James Island	7
Harbor View Elementary School	James Island	10
C. E. Williams Middle School for Creative and Science	James Island	7
Ashley River Creative Arts	West Ashley	10
Orange Grove Elementary Charter School	West Ashley	9
Springfield Elementary School	West Ashley	6
St. Andrews School of Math and Science	West Ashley	8
Stono Park Elementary School	West Ashley	5
Drayton Hall Elementary School	West Ashley	8
Sullivans Island Elementary School	Sullivan's Island	9
Haut Gap Middle School	Johns Island	7
Jennie Moore Elementary School	Mount Pleasant	10
Mt. Pleasant Academy	Mount Pleasant	10
Laing Middle School	Mount Pleasant	10
Moultrie Middle School	Mount Pleasant	10
Belle Hall Elementary School	Mount Pleasant	10
Charles Pinckney Elementary School	Mount Pleasant	10
Thomas C. Cario Middle School	Mount Pleasant	10
East Cooper Montessori Charter	Mount Pleasant	10
Mamie Whitesides Elementary	Mount Pleasant	9
James B. Edwards Elementary	Mount Pleasant	9
Buist Academy	Charleston	10
Charleston Charter for Math and Science	Charleston	8
Daniel Island School	Daniel Island	10

Only a handful of schools rank below average: One is in a rural area of John's Island, one is downtown, and the others are in North Charleston. Note that all three of these areas also have schools that rank well above average, and plenty of open conversations in the community show that the leadership and the teachers are committed to improving test scores and to giving kids the tools they need to do well. You can get a full list of school rankings by zip code or area at GreatSchools.org and see school report cards at the South Carolina State Department of Education's website.

A Night Off From the Kids

Since you'll be living in one of the most active and romantic cities in the country, you're going to want some adults-only time to explore. Because Charleston is such a friendly place, you'll likely find a trustworthy babysitter right in your new neighborhood, or meet other parents who are eager to swap babysitting duties. Otherwise, locals use Care.com or neighborhood teenagers when they need a date night. Average babysitting rates are $10.50 an hour. Some businesses and community organizations offer Parent's Night Out opportunities. At Black Tie Music Academy kids can have an evening of fun music instruction and activities while their parents take a break.

Fun Activities for Young Ones

Playing at the beach or in one of the many parks is a favorite pastime for kids, and there are plenty of shells, fossils and artifacts to hunt down on beaches and riverbanks. Young people and adults enjoy the South Carolina Aquarium. For a fun, hands-on history lesson the Children's Discovery Tour downtown is a great choice, as is the Children's Museum of the Lowcountry. Our waterparks are excellent fun in the summer, as are the many summer camps. Riverdogs Class A minor league baseball games take place in beautiful Joseph P. Riley, Jr. Park ("The Joe") and are geared for family frivolity. (Wait till you see the "bat dog" at work!) For evening fun, local theaters usually have at least one kid-friendly (pirate-themed) mystery play.

Animal lovers and their children will be fascinated at the Center for Birds of Prey in nearby Awendaw. This incredible facility rehabilitates owls, falcons, vultures, eagles and hawks—and their education programs are geared toward kids. Older children appreciate touring the civil war sites, but everyone enjoys the dolphin-filled ferry ride out to Fort Sumter.

College/Post High School

Charleston has an excellent array of colleges, universities and continuing education opportunities. Four-year colleges include The Citadel, College of Charleston (CofC) and Medical University of South Carolina (MUSC). Citadel cadets can take advantage of a recently expanded Fine Arts Department. This program offers he opportunity to study and appreciate fine art including painting, sculpture, photography, music, film, drama, and creative writing.

The College of Charleston offers a wide array of undergraduate degrees as well as 20 fascinating graduate degree options that include marine biology, historic preservation and African American studies.

MUSC graduate programs include PhD work in biomedical sciences, dual MD/PhD or DMD/PhD, and opportunities for post-doctoral research.

Trident Technical has two-year degree programs in 12 areas of study. Charleston School of Law prepares Lowcountry lawyers for their careers. And, the two-year Culinary Institute of Charleston is where budding Charleston chefs go to learn their chops.

There are eight private four-year colleges, including the Art Institute of Charleston, Charleston Southern University and Southern Wesleyan University, and three for-profit universities including Strayer University, ECPI University and Virginia College. Vocational colleges include the Academy of Cosmetology, American College of the Building Arts, Charleston Cosmetology Institute, Charleston School of Massage, Real Estate School of Charleston and Real Estate School of South Carolina.

Student Housing

Living downtown is one of the many perks of going to college in Charleston

Students at nearby universities have fun living and studying in historic downtown Charleston. Although there is some on-campus housing, off-campus housing is a popular choice because there are opportunities for affordable housing in historic homes and buildings. College of Charleston has a list of available student rentals and sublets, as does Apartment Finder. "Don't spend your best years in a dorm that cramps your style" is the motto of 400 Meeting Street, a downtown option for luxury student living. Also check out Sterling Campus Center Apartments for luxury CofC digs. MUSC has a nice list of housing options and include a roommate search option.

Community Education Classes

Some great opportunities for music education include Hungry Monk in West Ashley, Charleston Academy of Music downtown and Black Tie Music Academy on Daniel Island, in Park West, Summerville, Charleston, Mount Pleasant and in West Ashley. Charleston County Community Education hosts diverse opportunities for kids and adults year round, as does the Charleston County Public Library and local community centers. If you'd like to educate your furkids, the Charleston Animal Society holds regular dog training classes, as well as educational summer camps for kids and budding veterinarians. The exciting new Creative Arts of Mount Pleasant (CAMP) offers creative art classes for kids, including plenty of half-and full day programs to keep kids busy during summer break and on teacher work days. The art center also offers day, evening and weekend classes, open studios, lectures, and workshops for adults.

CHAPTER 10

MAKING FRIENDS AND GETTING INVOLVED

Can you make new friends here? Yes! The best way to make friends in Charleston is to just be friendly—it will be returned with gusto! In fact, in 2016 Travel + Leisure readers voted Charleston the Friendliest City in America. A good way to start meeting people and building relationships is to get involved in volunteer activities. There are local causes for nearly every interest, and Charlestonians will make you feel welcome right away.

Associations & Social Ties

There are some exceptional groups in our community that are examples of the interesting and important social endeavors taking place in the Lowcountry. The Charleston Port and Seafarers Society serves the basic needs of men and women who make their living on the many container ships that visit our ports. Some of these workers don't speak English, have been away from home for many months at a time, and are lonely or afraid. This group helps them make phone calls, provides rides to shopping areas and to medical appointments.

Charlestonians are oh-so-proud of the Charleston Animal Society, the only no-kill animal shelter in the Southeast and a model for other animal shelters around the country. Volunteers can walk dogs, take adoptable animals out to social events clad in "Adopt Me" jackets, feed and foster puppies and kittens or just provide safe havens in which injured animals can rest and heal. The shelter is a bright, clean, happy place staffed with well-organized, wildly intelligent people who are very good at regularly accomplishing the impossible.

**Taking a shelter dog for a social outing
is a great way to meet new friends.
Photo courtesy Charleston Animal Society**

Want to be part of sea turtle conservation efforts? Join the Island Turtle Team of Sullivan's Island or Isle of Palms, or the Folly Beach Turtle Watch team. Volunteers walk the beaches early in the mornings, recording the location of new nests, moving nests if necessary and educating the public about turning lights out during nesting season, filling in holes after playing on the beach (baby turtles fall in and can't get out), and picking up trash.

If history is your thing, be sure to join the Preservation Society of Charleston, the oldest community-based historic preservation organization in America.

These four organizations are a very small sampling of the unique volunteer activities available in Charleston. There are many other charitable organizations in the Lowcountry that serve women, at-risk children, the homeless population, animals and the environment.

**Gleaning extra crops for local food banks is a popular
social and philanthropic activity
Photo courtesy Lisa Isaacson**

You can find a list of Charleston nonprofits at GreatNonProfits.org.

The Coastal Community Foundation Makes High Impact in the Lowcountry

**The Coastal Community Foundation matches donors with non-profits
Courtesty Coastal Community Foundation**

Founded in 1974, Coastal Community Foundation empowers individuals, families, and organizations to make a lasting impact through permanent, endowed funds for charitable giving. We foster philanthropy for the lasting good of the community and are happy to help newcomers to Charleston get acquainted with the wide variety of philanthropic options here in the Lowcountry. The city of Charleston is a very special place and we consider ourselves lucky to call it our home. At Coastal Community Foundation, we provide an avenue for anyone and everyone to get involved with a community cause that they support. Whether you're interested in setting up a fund or donating to an existing nonprofit, we welcome you to be a part of creating lasting community impact.

Other good choices include:

Palmetto Medical Initiative – Provides sustainable, quality healthcare to those in need.

PetHelpers – No-kill animal shelter and adoptions.

Charleston Library Society – Research, preservation and lending library.

Charleston Habitat for Humanity – Works in partnership with people in need to build decent, affordable housing.

Charleston Rotary – Professionals dedicated to humanitarian service and world peace.

To Stay Current and Connected in Charleston Tune in to Local Media

Radio

WSCI – South Carolina Educational TV Radio [89.3 MHz] – NPR News and Classical

WKCL – We Know Christ Lives [91.5 MHz] – Contemporary Christian

WCKN – Kickin' 92.5 [92.5 MHz] – Country music

WWWZ – Z93 Jamz [93.3 MHz] – Urban Contemporary

WSCC – NewsRadio94.3 [94.3 MHz] – News / Talk

WSSX – 95SX [95.1 MHz] – Contemporary Top 40

WMXZ – Greatest Hits 95.9 [95.9 MHz] – Country music

WIWF – The Wolf [96.9 MHz] – Country

WYBB – 98X [98.1 MHz] – Active Rock

WWIK -ESPN [98.9 MHz] – Sports

WSPO – The Box [99.3 MHz] – Urban Contemporary

WXST – Star99.7 [99.7 MHz] – Urban Adult Contemporary

WALC – HIS Radio [100.5 MHz] – Contemporary Christian

WAYA-FM – WAY-FM [100.9 MHz] – Contemporary Christian

WAVF – CHUCK FM [101.7 MHz] – Adult Hits

WXLY – Y102.5 [102.5 MHz] – Adult Contemporary

WEZL – WEZL 103.5 [103.5 MHz] – Country

WRFQ – Q104.5 [104.5 MHz] – Classic Rock

WCOO – The Bridge @ 105.5 [105.5 MHz] – Album Adult Alternative

WJNI – Gospel 106.3 [106.3 MHz] – Gospel

WMGL – 107-3 MAGIC [107.3 MHz] – Urban Adult Contemporary

WLTQ – [730 kHz] – Black Gospel

WTMZ – The Team [910 kHz] – Sports Talk (ESPN Radio)

WJKB – AM 950 Classic Hit Country [950 kHz] – Classic Country

WAZS – El Sol [980 kHz] – Spanish

WTMA – The Lowcountry's Big Talker [1250 kHz] – News / Talk

WQSC – The Boardwalk [1340 kHz] – Beach Music

WIOP – The Box [1390 kHz] – Urban Contemporary (Simulcast on 99.3 FM)

WQNT – [1450 kHz] – Sports Talk (Fox Sports Radio)

WZJY – [1480 kHz] – Talk

101

Television

WCBD-TV – NBC Channel 2

WCIV-TV – ABC Channel 4

WCSC-TV – CBS Channel 5

WITV-TV – PBS Channel 7

WLCN-CD – Christian Television Network Channel 18

WTAT-TV – Fox Channel 24

WMMP-TV – MyNetWorkTV Channel 36

WHDC – Independent Channel 12

WCBD – NBC Channel 14

WCHD-TV – 4ABC Channel 9

Magazines

Carolina Tails Magazine

Charleston Living Magazine

Charleston Style & Design Magazine

Charleston Magazine

Charleston Weddings Magazine

LowCountry Dog

Lowcountry Parent

Mount Pleasant Magazine

Skirt Magazine

Newspapers

Post and Courier – daily newspaper

Catalyst – MUSC

Charleston City Paper – news & entertainment weekly

Charleston Currents – online – published twice-weekly

Charleston Mercury – conservative bimonthly

Charleston Regional Business Journal – biweekly business newspaper

Daniel Island News

Island Eye News – Sullivan's Island

James Island Messenger – published weekly

Moultrie News – Mount Pleasant

Summerville Journal Scene – published twice-weekly

Voting

South Carolina law requires you to register to vote at least 30 days before the election. There is no length of residency requirement in South Carolina in order to register to vote. You can register to vote or check your registration and eligibility at SCVotes.org. In order to vote you must have one of the following Photo IDs:

- SC Driver's License

- SC Department of Motor Vehicles ID Card

- SC Voter Registration Card with Photo

- Federal Military ID

- US Passport

CHAPTER 11

PRACTICAL NOTEBOOK ON MOVING

Moving Calendar

Anytime is a good time to move to Charleston. Practically speaking, moving in the middle of July heat and humidity combined with the extra tourist traffic may result in a day you'll laugh about later. But don't let it stop you from getting here as soon as possible. Do note that college students start to move in downtown late July and early August, so plan for patience if you're moving downtown in that time frame. If you're a college student, think about moving at the beginning of summer. You'll have a whole quarter to explore your new home and you'll avoid the moving rush.

Moving Tips & Assistance

If you're planning on doing your own move, here are some things to consider about Charleston:

- Many houses and apartments are elevated or "on stilts" due to flooding and building regulations. It's very likely that your new home will have several flights of stairs. Label your boxes clearly so movers can put them in their new rooms and you can just unpack. It's no fun hauling heavy boxes from the ground-level garage to the third-level master bedroom by yourself.

- It's hot and humid in the late spring, summer and into early fall. It's best to get help to get the truck unloaded as quickly as possible. Then you can take your time unpacking in the air conditioning.

- Many streets in Charleston are narrow and require expertise to safely navigate a moving van. Unless you're used to driving a big vehicle in a major city, backing up a truck down a historic alley is not something you want to try.

Do You Still Need All That Stuff?

Moving is a great time to lighten up your belongings, and moving to Charleston is an especially good opportunity to streamline; houses tend to be smaller, there are less storage opportunities and life is just simpler.

Decorating Your New Home: What to Bring, What to Sell

Many of our design clients who move to Charleston come to us and say "Nothing from our old home fits here!" Charleston has its own unique blend of interior styles ranging from elegant downtown antebellum mansions, to the salt box style island cottages of Isle of Palms and Sullivan's Island. It also has neighborhoods with "Neo-traditional homes" built

Photo courtesy Jennifer Patterson

to emulate downtown homes boasting double porches and layers of interior trim. So the question is, what should you bring when you come to town? While Charleston is a coastal town, going native does not mean going nautical. Lowcountry style is elegant and simple, reflecting a life spent along the coast fishing, boating and hunting. This hot climate requires a palette of lighter colors and fabrics that soothe the senses. Linen fabrics, old wood tables, white-slipcovered sofas and sea grass rugs work well with many interiors here. Don't bring any of your large overstuffed furniture, leather sofas, or dark wool rugs—you'll have a better chance selling them on consignment in your own city. I often use outdoor fabrics on my client's living room sofas, which allows them to enjoy white sofas, along with their children, grandchildren and dogs, with all the durability and none of the mess. Outdoor/indoor entertaining is an essential part of the Lowcountry lifestyle. Trade in your real wicker furniture (which will rot outside) for quality resin wicker or teak furniture. Bring your linens and china- you will be entertaining "al Fresco" on your wonderful piazzas, or porches if you live off the Peninsula. Charlestonians love their antiques and heirlooms, but by mixing them in with more modern pieces you can create a fresh twist on the traditional, without feeling stuffy or pretentious.

Jennifer Patterson, interior designer and owner of Terra Designs

Storage

One very important thing to keep in mind is that Charleston homes may not have the storage you're used to. First, because of the low geography and possibility of flooding, we don't have basements. Second, we do have attics but the heat and humidity make it impossible to safely store anything there. Third, we do have garages but the salt air quickly rusts metal and molds fabric and paper. If you have precious things to store, it's best to do it inside the house or rent a climate-controlled storage unit. If you're moving to an elevated house with the garage underneath, most insurance companies require garage walls to be louvered instead of solid so water can pass through during a flood. Whatever you store in your garage will effectively be exposed to the outside. Also, extreme high tides and heavy rains associated with tropical storms or hurricanes can flood garages. You won't want anything that can't be replaced stored on the floor. Though this sounds like a major mental adjustment, most people end up appreciating a reason to keep the garage tidy.

Space

Houses in Charleston tend to be smaller than many other areas of the country. If you have an enormous sectional sofa or a 70" TV, you may want to sell it and buy something right-sized when you get here.

Things to sell or donate:

- Winter coats, boots, hats and gloves
- Heavy sweaters
- Snow shovels and blowers
- Sleds, skis and snowboards unless you'll travel for snow vacations
- Dark clothes
- Clothes that aren't made of natural fibers
- Dark linens and furnishings
- Oversized furniture
- Flashy dress clothes (with the exception of one or two black-tie suits or cocktail dresses)
- Extras of anything except linens and beach towels

Things to bring:

- Light cotton and linen clothing
- Compact, light colored furniture
- Bicycles and outdoor fun gear
- Ladders and tools
- Light sweaters, sweatshirts or fleece jackets

Transportation & Logistics

Charleston lies east of the curvy Blue Ridge Mountains and south and north of the traffic snarls of many major cities. If you have to drive through them on your move, it may be worth hiring a transport company instead of trying to tow your car or boat yourself.

U-Haul has a fantastic service that arranges for strong helpers to meet you on the receiving end of the move. Their hourly rates are low and completely worth it, especially if you're moving in a hot month or into an elevated house. These guys and girls are usually hardworking college students, and it's hospitable to offer them cold drinks and nice tips when they're done. Just ask about the service when you rent your truck.

If you're temporarily moving to a small rental, you absolutely must have a climate-controlled storage unit or you risk raising the door on moldy furniture and boxes when you're ready to move to your permanent home.

Local Moving Companies:

Sure Load Moving – 843-971-1779

Uhaul at 584 King Street – 843-723-1605

All My Sons Moving & Storage – 843-480-4040

Smooth Move – 843-860-9717

PODS Charleston – 877-770- 7637

Climate-controlled Storage:

Pack Rat Self-Storage – Clean, well-lit, convenient locations in Mount Pleasant– 843-881-1250 and North Charleston–843 569-3100. Properties are cheerful and well kept.

Public Storage – Global chain with many locations and frequent online discounts. Several West Ashley locations–1-800-688-8057.

Uncle Bob's Self Storage – Mount Pleasant and Summerville, always gets good customer reviews – 800-242-1715.

Smart Stop Self Storage – No credit card deposit required, keyless entry so you don't have to keep track of a key. Mount Pleasant only– 843-849-1888.

Carter's City Self Storage – Downtown Charleston, 10% web discount. – 843-606-1591.

Sofa Won't Fit? Where to Donate

If you find you have household items to donate after your move, there are plenty of opportunities to get a tax break or make some cash:

Charleston Habitat for Humanity ReStore – 843-579-0777

Charleston Craigs List – CharlestonCraigsList.org

Palmetto Goodwill – 843-566-0072

CHAPTER 12
THE ECONOMY

Source of Vitality

It's an exciting time to live in Charleston. We rebounded quickly after the economic troubles of the last few years and there is every indication that Charleston is going through another renaissance. According to the 2015 Regional Economic Scorecard published by the Regional Development Alliance, Charleston's economy is performing better than the rest of the state, and the U.S. overall. Employment has grown twice as fast as the rest of the U.S. in the last three years, unemployment is lower than the national average, and jobs lost during the recession have been recovered.

Manufacturing, the medical industry, the military, tourism and the Ports Authority are the main drivers of Charleston's economy.

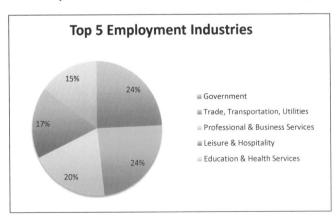

Top 5 Employment Industries

- Government — 24%
- Trade, Transportation, Utilities — 24%
- Professional & Business Services — 20%
- Leisure & Hospitality — 17%
- Education & Health Services — 15%

Efforts to Diversify the Economy

Information Technology

There is a strong push to create world-class centers for IT and IT security, aerospace and aviation, biomedical research, and renewable energy. Known as the "Silicon Harbor", Charleston's burgeoning tech industry is in the top 10 fastest growing cities in the U.S. for software and Internet technologies. And the Silicon Harbor is creating jobs and spawning IT and engineering start-ups faster than the local job market can supply workers.

The mothership in the harbor is the Charleston Digital Corridor, an expansive effort to grow the city's "knowledge economy". Also of interest is the Harbor Entrepreneur Center, an aggressive and well-organized program that mentors and grows start-ups. According to the Milken Institute, Charleston ranks alongside San Fransico, Austin, and Raleigh as #12 in the nation for high tech GDP growth.

Aircraft Mechanics and Engineers

Thanks to Boeing, Charleston is also the fastest growing mid-size metro for aircraft manufacturing and a top-ten contender for the highest workforce growth for aircraft mechanics and electrical engineers.

Biomed

MUSC makes Charleston a hotbed for the biomedical market. The city is home to more than 35 medical device and pharmaceutical manufacturers, and more than 50 research laboratories and development companies.

Renewable Energy

You may be surprised to learn that South Carolina is ranked the second highest U.S. state for wind energy manufacturing. You'll find the world's largest Wind Turbine Drivetrain Testing Facility in Charleston, and a growing marketing for "clean jobs".

Largest Public Sector Employers

In the public sector, the military is Charleston's largest employer. MUSC and Charleston's schools are a close second.

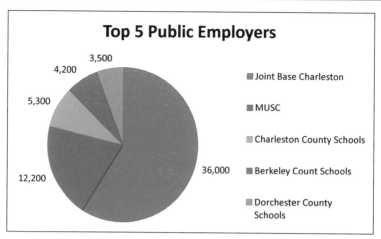

Source: Center for Business Research, Charleston Metro Chamber of Commerce

Largest Private Sector Employers

In the private sector, Boeing leads the way followed by healthcare, restaurants, and retail.

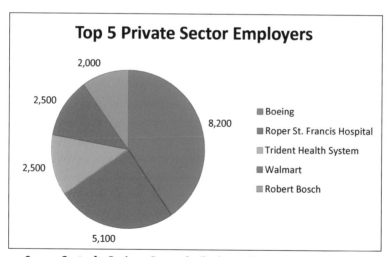

Source: Center for Business Research, Charleston Metro Chamber of Commerce

Headquarters & Branches

Charleston is home to many national and global corporate headquarters:

COMPANIES HEADQUARTERED IN CHARLESTON

COMPANY	INDUSTRY
ArborGen LLC	Tree genetics
AstenJohnson, Inc.	Manufacturing
Belimed, Inc.	Biomed
Benefitfocus	Software
Berchtold Corp.	Medical equipment
Blackbaud, Inc.	Software
Bunch Transport Inc.	Logistics
Call Experts	Call center
Cullum Mechanical Construction	Construction
Evening Post Industries Inc.	Media, real estate and forestry
GEL Group	Environmental
Giant Cement Holding Inc.	Construction
Hagemeyer North America	Construction
Hill-Rom Inc.	Medical equipment
JW Aluminum	Flat-rolled aluminum
Knight's Companies	Construction
Le Creuset of America	Cookware
Life Cycle Engineering Inc.	Engineering and technology
Mediterranean Shipping Co.	Manufacturing
Modulant	Software
MWV	Specialty chemicals
Pegasus Steel	Steel fabrication
PeopleMatter	Software
Quoizel, Inc.	Lighting
Rogers & Brown Custom Brokers & International Freight Forwarders	Logistics
Sawgrass Technologies	Specialty ink systems
SPARC, LLC	Software
The Intertech Group Inc.	Holding company for technology-driven manufacturing firms
The Urban Electric Co.	Lighting
Thrace-LINQ, Inc.	Textiles
TRUMPF Medical Systems, Inc.	Medical equipment
TWL Precision	Manufacturing
Ware On Earth Communications Inc.	IT
Z Marine of North America Inc.	Rigid-hull inflatable boats (RIBs)

Source: Charleston Regional Development Alliance

Why Companies Come to Charleston

Charleston's leadership is committed to continued economic diversification and growth. Businesses with branches or headquarters in the tri-county area will find plenty of support and financial opportunities. The natural beauty, fascinating history, quality of life and friendly atmosphere make Charleston an attractive draw for highly skilled employees.

Entrepreneurial Pursuits

Charleston's government and business leaders have made it clear: Entrepreneurs, start-ups and growing businesses are more than welcome here. Entrepreneurs will find plenty of like-minded individuals, networking opportunities and community support— regardless of their industry. Entrepreneurs in the tech industry can attend regular networking events put on by the Digital Corridor and the Harbor Accelerator. Techies should plan to attend the annual DigSouth festival, a five-day event that celebrates technical innovation and the digital economy.

Employment Market

The average worker in Charleston makes $44,800 per year, a figure that jumps to $72,000 if you are a technology worker.

At 4.3%, Charleston's unemployment rate is below the national average, and predicted to continue on a steady decline as employment growth well outpaces the state and national rates.

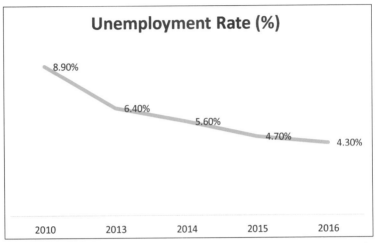

Source: U.S. Bureau of Labor Statistics

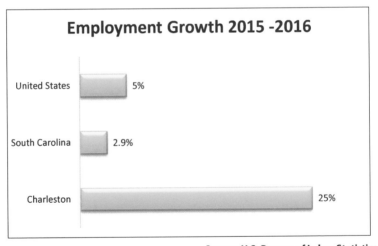

Source: U.S. Bureau of Labor Statistics

Charleston Occupation and Wages

OCCUPATION TITLE	HOURLY AVERAGE	ANNUAL AVERAGE	HOURLY MEDIAN	ANNUAL MEDIAN
All Occupations	$20.94	$43,555	$16.52	$34,361
Architecture & Engineering	$35.48	$73,798	$34.63	$72,030
Arts, Design, Entertainment, Sports & Media	$20.70	$43,056	$17.84	$37,107
Building & Grounds Cleaning / Maintenance	$11.34	$23,587	$10.21	$21,236
Business & Financial Operations	$31.18	$64,854	$28.54	$59,363
Community & Social Services	$21.83	$45,406	$19.98	$41,558
Computer & Mathematical	$36.00	$74,880	$34.57	$71,905
Construction & Extraction	$18.74	$38,979	$17.25	$35,880
Education, Training & Library	$23.64	$49,171	$22.70	$47,216
Farming, Fishing & Forestry	$16.38	$34,070	$15.30	$31,824
Food Preparation & Serving Related	$10.54	$21,923	$9.20	$19,136
Healthcare Practitioners & Technical	$34.31	$71,364	$29.20	$60,736
Healthcare Support	$13.68	$28,454	$12.89	$26,811
Installation, Maintenance & Repair	$21.37	$44,449	$20.17	$41,953
Legal	$31.45	$65,416	$23.85	$49,608
Life, Physical & Social Science	$29.38	$61,110	$26.72	$55,577
Management	$47.20	$98,176	$41.51	$86,340
Office & Administrative Support	$16.81	$34,964	$15.30	$31,824
Personal Care & Service	$11.47	$23,857	$9.80	$20,384
Production	$19.71	$40,996	$18.25	$37,960
Protective Service	$18.07	$37,585	$17.07	$35,505
Sales & Related	$15.27	$31,761	$10.77	$22,401
Transportation & Material Moving	$16.26	$33,820	$14.18	$29,494

Economic Indicators

According to the Charleston Regional Development Alliance's 2015 Economic Scorecard, Charleston's economy is strong and getting stronger.

GRP = A Strong Local Economy

The Gross Regional Product is an indicator of how much money is flowing through the area. Our GRP is 18.7%, falling just below the national average—that means there is money in the local economy.

Export Activity = People Spend Money Here

Export Activity measures how much money people all over the world spend on Charleston goods and services. Our Export Activity is $4 billion, a number that continuously rises, and puts us in the Top 100 Metros in the country.

Regional Employment = There Are Jobs Here

Regional Employment data measures the number of people who are actively employed. Between 2005 to 2014 our jobs rose by 17.4%. That rate is double and triple the state and U.S. figures.

Average Annual Pay Growth = Growing Community Wealth

Charleston's average annual pay grew to $41,944 between 2005 and 2013, which outperforms the state of South Carolina and the United States on the whole.

CONCLUSION

Is Charleston really all that? You don't have to take my word for it. Read any "Best of" list and you're likely to find us. Poke around on TripAdvisor and wade through thousands of gushing reviews, or visit local Facebook pages and see exiles lament that they aren't here right now. Yes, Charleston is all that and more. Whether you've lived here five days or fifty years you'll share a sense of awe, blessing and wonder with the rest of us.

What's it like to live here? Well, come sit at Red's on Shem Creek with us and let Monday's stress melt away as the dolphins play at sunset. Tuesday, let's walk the dogs on the beach before work. Have a good lunch on Wednesday because we're racing sailboats in the harbor later. You can rest up Thursday with tomato sandwiches on the porch, but don't stay late at work on Friday because we're dressing up for the Art Walk downtown. Are you going to the beach or the Farmer's Market Saturday? Well, whatever you do, don't make plans Sunday afternoon; we've saved you a seat at brunch.

I know…moving to a new city can't be based entirely on dreams and emotions (or can it?). Practically speaking, Charleston's economy is on fire. High-tech jobs are moving here faster than most of us can keep track, retail is booming and keeping pace with an incredibly successful tourism industry. There are jobs here, money is flowing into our community, schools are great and you may never make a better real estate investment in your life.

If that's not enough to convince you…we just got voted the Friendliest City in America by Condé Nast Traveler. So what are you waiting for? Go wash up, the tea's on the table, the biscuits are hot, and your new friends are waiting to meet you.

ABOUT THE AUTHOR

On a cold Indiana winter's day in 2012, Robin Howard and her husband William devised a two-year relocation plan to move to the ocean. They called a realtor, made a list of seaside possibilities, then spent the rest of the day planning a year of reconnaissance trips. Ten hours later they sold their house and had exactly eighteen days to move. Charleston was alphabetically first on the list, and the Howards had enjoyed some weekends in the Holy City, so they committed to a yearlong trial move. That move quickly became permanent as they fell hard for their new hometown—and discovered Robin's 10th great-grandfather, John Ashby, was one of the pioneers sent by King Charles II to settle Charleston in the 1600s.

The Howards put down roots in Mount Pleasant, just a few miles down the road from Quenby Plantation, Robin's family homestead. Today they are advocates for Charleston's historic, cultural, and ecological preservation, and support Charleston Animal Society's No Kill initiatives.

Robin is a member of the Charleston Ocean Racing Association and a working artist in the contemporary arts community. She is also a full-time freelance writer whose career spans more than 20 years. She regularly ghost writes for others and is a regular contributor to *Charleston Style & Design* and *Charleston Magazine* under her own byline. You can see more of her work at www.robinhowardwrites.com.

Robin is passionate about travel and enjoys sharing her favorite things about Charleston in her upcoming book and on her website: *Pluff Mud Pie: A Traveler's Guide to Unforgettable Days and Nights in Charleston.*

WEB LINKS AND EXTRAS

For the latest information about moving to and living in Charleston, please visit our companion website:
www.movingtocharlestonscguide.com

Important Contact Information and Web Links

Business Assistance:

Charleston Metro Chamber of Commerce
843 577 2510
www.charlestonchamber.net

Berkeley Chamber of Commerce
843-577-9549
www.berkeleysc.org/chamber

Dorchester Chamber of Commerce
843-873-2931
www.greatersummerville.org

Charleston Regional Development Alliance
843-767-9300
www.crda.org

Charleston Area Convention and Visitors Bureau
www.charlestoncvb.com

Charleston Area Maps
www.charlestoncvb.com/visitors/travel_support/maps.html

Cable and Telephone Services

Comcast
800-266-2278
www.comcast.com

AT&T
843-216-7063
www.att.com

Utilities

Electric & Gas
SCE&G
1-800-251-7234
www.sceg.com/

SCANA
www.scana.com

Garbage Collection

Charleston: (843) 724-7364

Folly Beach: (843) 588-2447

Isle of Palms: (843) 886-8956

James Island PSD: (843) 795-9060

Kiawah Island: (843) 768-9166

Mount Pleasant: (843) 884-8517

North Charleston: (843) 745-1026

Seabroook Island: (843) 768-9121

Sullivan's Island: (843) 883-3198

Recycling & Waste

Charleston County
(843) 720-2314
www.charlestoncounty.org/departments/SolidWaste

Dorchester County
843 832-0070
www.dorchestercounty.net

Berkeley County
(843) 572-4400
www.bcwsa.com

Water & Sewage

Charleston County
(843) 727-6800
www.charlestonwater.com

Dorchester County
(843) 563-0075
www.dorchestercounty.net

Berkeley County
(843) 572-4400
www.bcwsa.com

K-12 Education

Charleston County School District
843-937-6300
www.ccsdschools.com

Dorchester County – District 2
843-873-2901
www.dorchester2.k12.sc.us

Dorchester County – District 4
www.dorchester4.k12.sc.us

Berkeley County
(843) 723-4627
www.berkeley.k12.sc.us

Emergency

In an emergency, call 911.
In a boating emergency, hail the Coast Guard on channel 16

Government

Social Security
800-772-1213
www.ssa.gov

Tax Collector

843-958-4200
Charleston County
www.charlestoncounty.org/TaxInfo
Dorchester County
843-563-0162
www.dorchestercounty.net

Berkeley County
843-719-4030
www.berkeleycountysc.gov

Hospitals

MUSC
www.musc.edu
843-792-2300

East Cooper Medical Center
843-881-0100
www.eastcoopermedctr.com

Roper St. Francis
843-724-2000
www.rsfh.com

Bon Secours St. Francis
www.rsfh.com
843-402-1000

Police Non-emergency

843-308-4718

Sheriff

843-202-1700
www.ccso.charlestoncounty.org

Registrations and Licensing

BMV
SCDMV
803-896-5000.
www.scdmvonline.com/DMVpublic

Fishing
DNR
803-734-3833
www.dnr.sc.gov/purchase.html

Transportation

Air
Charleston International Airport
www.chs-airport.com
843-767-7000

Bus & DASH Trolley
CARTA
843-724-7420
www.ridecarta.com

SCDOT
www.dot.state.sc.us 843-740-1655

Books, Television Shows and Movies Set in Charleston

Books

The Prince of Tides by Pat Conroy
South of Broad by Pat Conroy
Beach Music by Pat Conroy
The Great Santini by Pat Conroy
The Lords of Discipline by Pat Conroy
My Losing Season by Pat Conroy
The Water is Wide by Pat Conroy
Bulls Island by Dorothea Benton Frank
Plantation by Dorothea Benton Frank
Sullivan's Island by Dorothea Benton Franks
Southern Fried Plus Six by William Price Fox
Edisto: a Novel by Padgett Powell
The Yemmessee: A Romance of Carolina by William Gilmore Simms
Bastard Out Of Carolina by Dorothy Allison
Celia Garth by Gwen Bristow
Charleston by John Jakes
The Secret Life of Bees by Sue Monk Kidd

The Mermaid Chair by Sue Monk Kidd
Where The River Runs by Patti Callahan Henry
When The Light Breaks by Patti Callahan Henry
Sweetgrass by Mary Alice Monroe
The Beach House by Mary Alice Monroe

Television

Southern Charm – Bravo Network reality show
Reckless – CBS
Army Wives – Lifetime
North and South, Love and War, Heaven & Hell: North & South,
Book III – Miniseries – The Hunley – TV movie

Popular Movies Filmed in Charleston

Ace Ventura: When Nature Calls

Die Hard with a Vengeance

The Legend of Bagger Vance

The Notebook

The Patriot

The Prince of Tides

White Squall

Cold Mountain

ACKNOWLEDGMENTS

Whether you're dreaming of finding the perfect seaside town and simplifying your life, or you're already enmeshed in the process of moving to Charleston and making a life here, with this book I endeavored to help you skate through the stressful stuff and get on with cocktails on Shem Creek. Fulfilling those intentions require far more skill than I will ever have on my own, so I would like to express my deep gratitude to everyone involved in helping me, and helping you. Special thanks to Jason Crichton of Jason Crichton Photography for getting up before dawn to capture our amazing cover photo. The biggest thanks goes to the Charleston community for being an unfailing example of how to behave, even in the worst circumstances.

CPSIA information can be obtained at www.ICGtesting.com
Printed in the USA
BVIW12n1225130217
476050BV00001B/6